MW01257931

Wild Ride

Wild Ride

A Journey of Transformation

—*A Memoir*

SHERILL L. HOSTETTER

RESOURCE *Publications* · Eugene, Oregon

Wild Ride
A Journey of Transformation—A Memoir

Copyright © 2022 Sherill L. Hostetter. All rights reserved. Except for brief quotations in critical publications or reviews, no part of this book may be reproduced in any manner without prior written permission from the publisher. Write: Permissions, Wipf and Stock Publishers, 199 W. 8th Ave., Suite 3, Eugene, OR 97401.

Resource Publications
An Imprint of Wipf and Stock Publishers
199 W. 8th Ave., Suite 3
Eugene, OR 97401

www.wipfandstock.com

PAPERBACK ISBN: 978-1-6667-4159-9
HARDCOVER ISBN: 978-1-6667-4160-5
EBOOK ISBN: 978-1-6667-4161-2

VERSION NUMBER 051222

Scripture quotations are from the New Revised Standard Version Bible, copyright © 1989 National Council of the Churches of Christ in the United States of America. Used by permission. All rights reserved worldwide.

Quotes from the book *The Gift of Being Yourself: The Sacred Call to Self-Discovery*, copyright © 2004 by David G. Benner. Reprinted with permission of InterVarsity Press, Madison, WI. www.intervarsity.org

To my children,
Obe, Rene, and Jodie,
Your stories are interwoven with my story,
And you are now creating your own life stories.
May you find on your journeys
deeper intimacy with the God of love,
freedom in being your true selves,
and purpose in risky love of others.

Contents

Preface

WE ARE PEOPLE FORMED by story, the stories we tell about God, the stories we tell about ourselves, and the stories we tell about the world. God has invited us to enter a story larger than ourselves and our human comprehension, a story of a God who is both known and mysterious. Yet, we as humans desire certainty in our understanding of God and ourselves, and how God will interact with us in life. We desire promises of security in every aspect of life.

We are all living with uncertainty due to the Covid pandemic, the crisis in Ukraine, climate change, and hearing daily of threats looming over our future. We are tempted to hold on fiercely to our certainty about God and ourselves. Learning to open ourselves to new perspectives feels scary for all of us. As a spiritual director over the last twenty-one years, I have walked with many on their own journeys of transformation. During the Covid pandemic, I felt an inner nudging to vulnerably share my story, including my doubts, questions, laments, and fears.

Although I have traveled to forty-five countries in my seventy years of life and experienced many meaningful stories to share, the deeper journey has been an internal one, a spiritual journey in relationship with God and my personal journey with self. My God image and self-image were upended by trauma. The certainty I knew in my faith unraveled into questions. Through experiences with Swazi colleagues over eleven years of living and serving in Swaziland, Southern Africa, I opened myself to learn new perspectives of God and myself. In hearing the heart-wrenching stories of pain caused by the Mozambican civil war and the risky challenges to end Apartheid in South Africa, I wrestled with how the promises of God related to those experiencing war and death.

As I learned to live within the love of God no matter the circumstances, my soul was shaped into a new creation. My transformed God image and self-image have brought freedom and opportunities I would not have dreamed possible.

You are invited to saddle your thoroughbred and take this wild ride with me. Your circumstances will be different from mine, but you may inwardly identify with the deeper processing of doubts and questions. Though your journey has taken you in different directions geographically, you'll most likely recognize the terrain: the open flatlands, steep mountains, deep valleys, and treacherous pathways. Come ride with me!

Preface

WE ARE PEOPLE FORMED by story, the stories we tell about God, the stories we tell about ourselves, and the stories we tell about the world. God has invited us to enter a story larger than ourselves and our human comprehension, a story of a God who is both known and mysterious. Yet, we as humans desire certainty in our understanding of God and ourselves, and how God will interact with us in life. We desire promises of security in every aspect of life.

We are all living with uncertainty due to the Covid pandemic, the crisis in Ukraine, climate change, and hearing daily of threats looming over our future. We are tempted to hold on fiercely to our certainty about God and ourselves. Learning to open ourselves to new perspectives feels scary for all of us. As a spiritual director over the last twenty-one years, I have walked with many on their own journeys of transformation. During the Covid pandemic, I felt an inner nudging to vulnerably share my story, including my doubts, questions, laments, and fears.

Although I have traveled to forty-five countries in my seventy years of life and experienced many meaningful stories to share, the deeper journey has been an internal one, a spiritual journey in relationship with God and my personal journey with self. My God image and self-image were upended by trauma. The certainty I knew in my faith unraveled into questions. Through experiences with Swazi colleagues over eleven years of living and serving in Swaziland, Southern Africa, I opened myself to learn new perspectives of God and myself. In hearing the heart-wrenching stories of pain caused by the Mozambican civil war and the risky challenges to end Apartheid in South Africa, I wrestled with how the promises of God related to those experiencing war and death.

As I learned to live within the love of God no matter the circumstances, my soul was shaped into a new creation. My transformed God image and self-image have brought freedom and opportunities I would not have dreamed possible.

You are invited to saddle your thoroughbred and take this wild ride with me. Your circumstances will be different from mine, but you may inwardly identify with the deeper processing of doubts and questions. Though your journey has taken you in different directions geographically, you'll most likely recognize the terrain: the open flatlands, steep mountains, deep valleys, and treacherous pathways. Come ride with me!

Acknowledgements

BEFORE WRITING THIS MEMOIR, I never fully understood the many hours and people involved in the writing and publishing of a book. I now recognize the privilege it is to have access to numerous books on almost any topic for our learning and reading pleasure.

I want to express my thanks to my spiritual director of many years, Sharon Kraybill, who listened to me beneath my words. She served as God's midwife for further transformation on my journey. My husband, Darrel, loved me through the whole journey, no matter the terrain, and without his encouragement and support, this story would not be written.

Thank you to family and friends who faithfully saved all the letters we sent from overseas, restoring to my memory details I would have forgotten. And thanks to the staff of the agency that sent us to Nigeria for offering us the archival documents relating to our experiences.

Special thanks to Alison Wearing of *Memoir Writing Ink* for the memoir writing course I took on-line. It inspired me to get started. And thanks to Joyce Hostetter, author of historical fiction children's literature, who gave me feedback that resulted in my learning to be a better writer. I am indebted to the people who read a draft of this book and gave me invaluable feedback. Thank you to my daughter, Rene Hostetter, for editing drafts of the manuscript and to Laura Miller, for copy editing the book.

Finally, thanks to the Wipf and Stock staff for accepting and publishing my memoir.

PART I

Learning Certainty, Experiencing Complexity and Perplexity

There is no deep knowing of self
without a deep knowing of God,
and no deep knowing of God
without a deep knowing of self.

—*The Gift of Being Yourself: The Sacred Call
To Self-Discovery* by David G. Benner

1

Spare My Son!

Nigeria, West Africa, 1980

PLEASE GOD, HELP HER get it on the first stick! I stroke the face of my son, Obe, and kiss his forehead in my attempt to soothe his suffering.

Helplessness overwhelms me, as I look deep into the sad eyes of my pale, listless, almost two-year-old son lying on his well-loved green blanket on our kitchen table in Aba, Nigeria. He barely whimpers in his stupor as the nurse from the nearby clinic sticks the needle into his arm and tapes it into place. I hang the IV bag on the crank of the upper louvre windows and fully open the IV valve, as I had done so often when I worked as a nurse earlier in life.

The clinic nurse gazes at Obe for a moment in silence. "We're remembering you," she whispers, touching my shoulder on her way out the door.

My husband, Darrel, and I stand over our son with pounding hearts, unabashedly grieving the loss of his playful self. I can picture Obe pushing his favorite toy around the yard five days ago, while I am washing cloth diapers by hand in a large basin. To others, this toy may appear like junk. To Obe, however, the handlebars and front wheel of a broken tricycle are a rare treasure. Obe's sheer delight in pushing the half tricycle demonstrates his new sense of accomplishment.

"God, please spare the life of our son!" Darrel cries out in a shaky voice while hugging my trembling body closer to him.

"I don't even know if God hears us anymore after all that has happened," I mutter.

"Are you sure we shouldn't drive him to the Port Harcourt hospital?" Darrel inquires.

I turn to face Darrel directly, staring into his eyes. "They will also start an IV to hydrate him, and it will take some time to do the testing and get results. We are out of time, Darrel. It's a four-hour drive to Port Harcourt, and he could die on the way there. I know what can happen when young children become this lethargic from dehydration!" I have been giving Obe a broad-spectrum antibiotic injection four times a day as the doctor ordered, trusting that we're treating Obe's unknown illness in the best possible way. I hope it is enough!

"If only we had a phone nearby so we could call family to ask them to pray with us," Darrel said.

"Yes, if only! You always say God will take care of us no matter what! Look what our life has been here, just continual crises and conflicts!" I rub the back of my neck to relieve the tension.

With tears stinging my eyes, I slump into a chair, letting out an exhausted sigh. Darrel leans down to give me a kiss on my forehead and then massages my shoulders. The last few days have been a blur. We are fighting a losing battle to keep our son alive as high fever, diarrhea, and vomiting continue to suck the life out of him.

I decide to keep watch during the night, as I won't be able to sleep anyway. It is only a matter of time before our newborn, Rene, will be hungry and need the nourishment only I can give her. Muted starlight shimmers through the louvre windows. Obe's serene face in the soft glow gives me a small glimmer of hope. My mind takes me back to our arrival in Nigeria.

*****

Arriving in Nigeria, Summer, 1979

One year prior to this stressful night, we had traveled from the United States to Kano, Nigeria. Obe had awoken with a fever of 104 degrees Fahrenheit the night before we were to leave Harrisonburg, Virginia, on the thirty-six-hour trip to Nigeria. Though I wanted to hold and cuddle him in my arms, I sponged his heat-radiating body in the bathtub while listening to his screams of terror at such shocking treatment.

"I will *not* travel with a sick child!" I said, hoping Darrel heard my emphasis on the word "not." How could we leave with a sick child?

"But I feel torn," Darrel said, "as we are planning to connect with people in Nigeria who will be waiting to help us through customs and ensure transportation at night from the Kano airport to Jos. I can't call them since they are enroute." We asked for counsel from others and finally decided to leave, trusting that whatever was causing the fever would be short lived. But, as a nurse, I felt foolish for taking such a risk.

The picture of Obe lying asleep in the child's hanging bassinet in front of our seats on the plane was imprinted in my memory. Sleep alluded me as I repeatedly touched his forehead, reassuring myself that he only had a low-grade fever. On our layover in Brussels, Belgium, we left a large stain on the airport carpet from Obe's bout of diarrhea. I wondered how many more times in this risky adventure we would leave our mark. We had signed up for three years as mission workers in Nigeria. Was this only a foreshadowing of things to come?

After landing in Nigeria and getting through customs, we slowly made our way out of the airport with our child and luggage. Ten Nigerian men pounced on our luggage to secure a tip for carrying it. In the scramble, two pieces of our luggage ended up being dumped on the pavement. We hurriedly stuffed our personal belongings back into the suitcases so we wouldn't hold up our arranged transportation. Darrel was at a loss of who to pay, so he gave the money to one man and let them haggle over dividing it.

As we traveled through the night to Jos, my soul was cloaked with anxiety for my sick one-year-old son and the many unknowns of the months ahead. I strained to see through the darkness out the window, taking mental pictures of the small, round mud huts with thatched roofs grouped together as compounds. The fear grew within me, as I doubted I would be able to adapt to life here. Even at night we were sweating in the hot, humid temperature.

At the guesthouse, instead of sleeping, we sponged Obe down again amidst his tired, resistant cries as his temperature had risen to 105 degrees. Beyond exhaustion, I dragged myself out of bed every few hours to do what needed to be done, torturing my precious son again.

Obe recovered within three days, but then I became sick with the virus.

*****

From Certainty to Complexity

Nigerians surrounded us wherever we traveled in the local area, touching my hair and skin, and trying to take Obe out of my arms. We were the only expatriates (white foreigners) in the district.

The principal of the school where Darrel was to teach chose three small rooms (imagine large walk-in closets) for us to live in behind the village chief's large house. They were part of an extended number of rooms surrounding a central concrete courtyard. The small rooms were built as the living quarters of the chief's multiple wives. There was no running water. A small tin shed served as an outhouse.

I knew I needed to give up a lot of comforts in Nigeria, but I hadn't expected to give up privacy in our own home. The chief's wives cooked over open fires in the courtyard. In my imagination, I could visualize Obe crawling around in the courtyard with open fires. I shuttered, repulsed by the idea of my son being so close to danger.

No one from the mission agency had made an administrative visit to prepare for us living and working in Nigeria. The Nigerian school principal and his wife had spent years in the United States, where he obtained his college and master's degrees with scholarships from the mission agency. Since the principal had lived in the United States, the agency trusted him to find adequate housing for us and orient us to the area. I could not understand why the principal would choose this type of housing for us if he cared about our well-being. My highest priority was the safety of my son.

So, we declined that housing option. However, I struggled with guilt for selfishly desiring to protect my son and needing a bit of privacy. *What was God really asking of me in this assignment? Am I just not strong enough to be here?* I wasn't sure I wanted to know the answers to my questions. Not now. . .maybe not ever.

We had noticed that it appeared common for some Nigerians to own individual block houses, and we had visited the principal's large block house. When we told the Nigerian church leaders that we could not accept their housing option, they bluntly instructed us to talk to the mission agency about building us a house. The principal said they did not want us to leave Nigeria without providing them with a guesthouse on the school property.

Our language tutor, Udoffa, a pastor in the church, later admitted to us, "The principal and the church leaders wanted you to be dissatisfied with the housing situation they offered you so you would pressure the agency to build you a house on our school compound."

So, we are pawns to be used in obtaining more buildings for them funded by the mission agency. And our comfort and care in arriving as guests in their country is not their priority. No wonder they were not motivated to help us find other housing options.

"Thanks, Udoffa, for your explanation. It was exceedingly difficult for us to decline what we were offered since we didn't want to offend anyone," Darrel said.

We felt the pressure to find an adequate place to live, as we had been temporarily living with a Lutheran mission family about a two-hour drive from the Nigerian school for the three weeks since our arrival. The wife had sprained her ankle during our stay with them, so she was appreciative of my cooking and cleaning. She read many books to Obe on the couch with her swollen foot propped up. This couple became wonderful friends to us, even though at age twenty-seven and twenty-six on our arrival, we could have been their children.

Eventually, we rented a house in a neighboring village of the school. The village chief had been using it as an office. The local Lutheran Church, as well as the village, claimed ownership of the house. The church leaders assured us they would work out rightful ownership issues without involving us. They admitted it should have been done long ago, so they released us to negotiate with the village elders about renting the house in the meantime. After going back and forth on a rental price, we reached an agreement with the village elders. The house was in disrepair. We spent many days scrubbing black mold off walls, fixing a leaking roof, and preparing to move in while our Lutheran mission friends cared for Obe. Headaches plagued me in cleaning the house, which often happens when I am exposed to fungus, mold, or dust mites. I thought I could not complain about the mold, though, because I was the one who said I couldn't live in the three small rooms with little privacy. This was at least a house!

We felt fortunate that there was a stream thirty yards downhill from the house where we could collect water. I had difficulty carrying heavy containers of water uphill from the stream since I had not yet learned the Nigerian skill of carrying water on my head. Therefore, Darrel often carried the water from the stream up the hill to our repaired cistern. I then pumped water into our kitchen. We boiled our drinking water to ensure it was safe.

The chief's wives walked on the path from our house to the stream to wash clothes, take baths, or carry water back to their compound. They wore colorful printed wraparound skirts but were naked from the waist up. "*Emedi*!" the women at the stream would greet Darrel with wide smiles and gestures. To Darrel, the greetings seemed laced with a bit of humor. We learned later from our Lutheran friends that it was culturally taboo for a man to carry water for a woman. I practiced greeting the women walking to the stream. Their smiles gave me hope that someday I could have more of a conversation with them.

We moved in before the house was ready because I was now pregnant, and we felt a need to become more settled. Schools were opening and Darrel needed to be ready to teach at the school, as well as serve as vice principal. Whenever Obe played outside, many Nigerian children surrounded him. If a toy was out of his reach, the children immediately brought it back to him. In the mornings, we often found Obe in his bed looking out his open window jabbering away in unintelligible language to children gathered outside.

In the hot and humid temperatures, washing sheets, towels, and diapers by hand took a lot of time. I hired people to help with the household chores, but they often did not last long. Either they needed to leave to plant their own seasonal crops in another area of the country or there was an emergency that demanded their attention. One young man, who cut our grass with a machete, knocked on my door one day. He was cutting grass around the six-to-eight-feet-high ant hills dotted across our front yard. Holding up a large ant larva, he asked, through hand motions, if I wanted to eat this delicacy. When I declined, he leaned his head back, dropped the larva into his mouth, and smiled with gratification. *I'd rather eat chocolate, thank you.* Chocolate was one luxury in the United States I craved.

One day, I discovered a bat flying around our living room after hearing Obe laughing with delight at the unusual entertainment. I had no idea how to get the bat out of the house. While waiting for Darrel to return home, I kept track of where it was to prevent being attacked. On his arrival, Darrel took up the challenge. Obe and I squealed with laughter as Darrel ran around the room waving a badminton racket in futile attempts to get the bat out of the house. He looked like a cat trying to catch a laser beam. Eventually the bat decided to leave the chaos and flew outside through the open door.

I learned quickly to discern Obe's screams of terror when he accidentally stepped into a line of army ants. I would drop everything and run to rescue him. The large black ants, the size of the smallest beetles, crawled up Obe's leg and chest, across his head, and down his opposite leg before continuing their straight line on the ground. Obe froze like a statue with his mouth open in a continuous scream until I could rescue him and treat the painful bites of the army ants. I cried in seeing Obe covered with red, raised welts because I couldn't protect him.

There was no way to contact Darrel while he was at the school all day, as telephones weren't available. I had to learn to deal with whatever situation arose. One day, I threw something in the trash can in the kitchen and discovered a large, moving, green snake tail. The rest of its body was under a three-foot-long cupboard beside the trashcan. Snakes could enter the house under the outside doors that were an inch off the floor.

Could this possibly be a green mamba? It's the most dangerous snake in Africa! Oh, God, what do I do? My motherly instinct overrode my paralysis. I knew that Obe couldn't be protected inside the house unless I dealt with the snake. After placing Obe in a safe area he couldn't leave, I wiped my clammy hands on my skirt, took a deep breath, and ran outside to the shed to grab the machete, a flashlight, and a thick wooden pole.

Crouching down on the floor, I shone the flashlight under the cupboard to locate exactly where the four-foot snake was lying. I jammed the stick under the cupboard as hard as I could, pinning the snake. *Now to hold it steady!* The snake's head stuck out the left side of the cupboard, its tongue flicking in and out in a rhythmic pattern. I grabbed the machete with my left hand, took aim, and cut off the snake's moving head, kicking it out the door. When my brain finally focused on Obe's cries, I picked him up and snuggled him close. My mind kept racing, though, refusing to rest.

This scenario could have ended differently! What if the snake would have struck while I crouched down on the floor? What if the pole I jammed under the cupboard would have missed? I didn't want to imagine what could have happened!

When Darrel arrived home, he found a Nigerian neighbor to verify what kind of snake I had killed. Indeed, it was a green mamba.

I told Darrel that our goal of living in Nigeria for ten years seemed beyond my capabilities. We had no time for concentrated language learning before Darrel was expected to teach school. Leaving the house with a small child to find persons to practice language with didn't happen as I had imagined. Daily life was difficult and time consuming with washing sheets and clothes by hand, grinding peanuts into peanut butter, and cooking everything from scratch without many ingredient options. Cooking while pregnant with palm nut oil created smells that left me nauseated. So, after cooking supper, I often couldn't eat it. The only "green vegetables" I could find to include in my cooking were pumpkin leaves. Dried fish that we bought at the market served as the protein in our diet. Sometimes we would buy meat at the market in a larger city. We would go early in the morning to ensure it was fresh. If the liver or other cut of meat was still quivering, we were assured of its freshness.

Through new challenges, I kept trying to adapt, but the loneliness of being isolated without a telephone or transportation increased over time. As an extrovert, I kept crying out to God to help me learn how to appreciate the solitude. I attempted to build relationships with some of the chief's many wives, but it was difficult as I hadn't learned much of the Efik language and they didn't speak any English. After some months, I craved to be able to talk with someone in English.

*****

The Conflict Escalates

Five months after our move into the house in the village, a Nigerian church representative for the Lutheran denomination appeared on our doorstep. He delivered a letter written by their lawyer. It stated they were taking us to court for paying rent to the village rather than to the Lutheran church. This was exactly what the church leaders assured us they would not do.

We talked to the village elders about resolving this conflict with the Lutheran Church. They responded by writing a letter to us stating they would evict us if we did not continue paying rent money to them. They later brought a copy of a letter they sent to the Nigerian authorities accusing us of being CIA agents, bringing division to the village, and abusing the poor. It was "signed" by the thumbprints of all the village elders. Later, one village elder, who was our friend, told Darrel we had better get out our gun. *Wow! How do we know who to trust as a newcomer to this country? What does friendship mean here?*

It was only a matter of time before the village elders might show up at our house to evict us. We had only lived in this house for six months, but we were expecting the birth of our second child in a month. Therefore, we felt pressured to find another place to live as quickly as possible. The principal of the school and the church leaders said they had no ideas for us. There were no housing options in the rural area near the school at that time.

Eventually, we found a house about an hour's drive from the school. We could only live there temporarily until after our baby was born. Our move took us to another Nigerian state, though, which also meant a different spoken language. The country of Nigeria has more than two hundred and fifty languages. We had been trying to learn the Efik language through the help of Udoffa, our private tutor. Now, we were hearing the Ibo language in our new location. I had the benefit, though, of talking to some people in English who lived nearby.

Three weeks later, two government personnel appeared at the school. They delivered a summons to Darrel and the principal to appear before the chair of the board of supervisors for the local government district. This summons was in response to the village elders' complaints against us. The chair told Darrel we should not be living in one Nigerian state while teaching in another. He also told the principal to find us adequate and permanent housing closer to the school. However, we did not hear anything further about housing from the principal.

2

More Questions and Complications

I GAVE BIRTH TO Miriam Rene during the night at the nearby clinic with the help of a midwife. My mother-in-law, who was visiting for a few weeks, joined Darrel and me in the birth experience at our invitation. She had given birth to eight children but had never been awake for any of the births.

The few birthing rooms were full, so I had no choice but to give birth on a table in a large room with glass windows without shades on two sides of the room. I tried to forget my desire for privacy as I laid naked on the table doing my Lamaze breathing exercises and staring at the bottles of medications on the shelves to distract myself. My breathing exercises mystified the Nigerian midwife. Darrel's desire to be with me for the birth surprised her as well since this was not the cultural norm.

I expected my labor for this second birth to be shorter than Obe's birth process, but I was in labor most of the night. Finally, when the first glimmer of morning sunlight shone into the windows, Rene's tiny vernix-coated body slithered out in a grand appearance with a hefty cry. I held Rene on my bare chest and kissed her wet black curls. *Thank you, thank you, thank you for a safe delivery, God!*

After handing our newborn to Darrel, I surveyed the room and discovered many eyes looking through the windows. As it turned light, students walking to school had discovered this "*Oyibo*" (foreign woman) lying naked on a table. In the intensity of giving birth, I was oblivious to their faces until that moment. I instinctively crossed my arms over my breasts, covering what I could. The midwife was massaging my abdomen for the placenta to release, so I had to forget about getting covered up. I turned my face away from the window, mortified in being that day's entertainment. *I'm sure this will be an exciting tale that will be repeated!* This is literally what it must mean "to be on display," like being in a car accident and people driving by slowly to gawk at you. Within an hour, we proudly took Rene home to meet her big brother.

When Nigerians came to visit our new baby, they marveled at Rene's beauty, as they were used to foreign white newborns looking pink. Rene did not conform to much of anything termed "normal." She gradually became increasingly jaundiced, evidenced in her eyes as well as her skin color. The nearby clinic didn't have the capacity to test for bilirubin, and there were no ultraviolet lights available (usual treatment for jaundice). Also, there was little sunlight to treat her jaundice naturally since it rained for twenty-six days in a row after she was born. It was an unusual rainy season.

The electric power went out the day after I gave birth. We couldn't use the toilet or take baths because our running water was connected to an electric pump on the clinic compound. Darrel and his father dug an open latrine pit out behind our house for our toileting business.

"First, I have the indignity of Nigerian children watching me give birth, and now they get to watch me poop? There aren't even any walls to hide behind," I grumbled to Darrel. But there was no other option. *Give me a break!*

Darrel and his father drove a few miles to find water for our drinking, cooking, and to wash the diapers and clothes. We drove forty miles to take infrequent showers at a friend's house. Darrel's mother washed diapers by hand for two babies every day and hung them around our house on furniture when it was raining. We do not know how we would have coped in those first weeks without Darrel's parents.

*****

Decisions Made Without Us

The impermanence of our housing situation and relationship struggles with the school principal dominated our thoughts and conversations. We felt pressure to make decisions.

Two weeks after my parents-in-law left, Darrel's younger brother, Phil, arrived. He had come to northern Nigeria to teach at an international school. Phil informed us that our mission agency had terminated our assignment and sent a telegram informing us and the school principal. We were now to join another church agency in northern Nigeria for a different assignment. Phil had driven a van down from Jos to move our essential belongings to the north. We knew nothing about this plan as we never received the telegram. Darrel gasped in shock. He stroked his beard repeatedly as though he might rub it off his face.

"How could the mission agency terminate us," Darrel lamented, "when we only asked them for counsel? They had inferred that someone would come to help us with the messiness of our situation. We didn't ask to be terminated. We are not quitters!"

Darrel strutted around the room while continuing to vent. "I can't believe they would do this! Most of the conflict and misunderstandings we've experienced here are a direct result of no one from the agency making an administrative visit prior to our assignment!"

"This is surreal!" I said to Phil while stacking the dirty dishes on the edge of the sink. "They made decisions without contacting us in person. And we've been waiting for five months for their promise that someone would come visit. This is the second place we have moved to in eight months and this one is temporary. As vice principal, Darrel travels an hour one way to go teach at the church's school. We've tried to keep going in this assignment. Do they even care what we think?"

I kicked Obe's ball across the room. "Now they just wash their hands by terminating us and handing us off to another agency? Why did we even come?" I asked, stalking out of the room. I had been holding on to hope that this situation could be turned around with the help of a third party. And we had waited a long time for the mission agency to get the message that we couldn't live in limbo indefinitely. Darrel and I had a difficult time going to sleep that night. Our emotions churned within us.

The next morning, my beautiful six-week-old baby began spitting up blood. That evening, she brought up two large blood clots. In a panic, I drove her to a doctor's house.

"What is happening to my baby?" I squeaked in a high-pitched voice as I showed him the evidence of the blood clots.

He replied in a forceful tone, "You need to leave early tomorrow morning for Jos. Your baby needs medical care beyond what we can offer. I don't want to be responsible for whatever is wrong. She needs tests to determine where this blood is coming from in her body."

Will this nightmare ever end? What am I doing wrong? Though I told myself that there was no time to feel anything, my heart felt constricted in fear. There was so much to do to be ready to leave by morning. Phil would drive Obe, Rene, and me to Jos while Darrel took a twelve-hour bus ride to the capital city of Lagos. Darrel would try to obtain a passport for Rene in case we needed to leave the country for more medical assistance. Though we were communicating with the mission agency through letters, Darrel would also call our mission agency supervisor while he was in Lagos where a phone was available. Darrel would later join the children and me in Jos. Another short night of sleep left us both emotionally on edge. We clung to each other, not wanting to say goodbye, not able to hold back the tears.

*****

Trip to Jos

The five-hundred-mile trip to Jos was intense. "Phil!" I yelled, "that driver almost collided with the one coming around the corner!" The driver honked his horn continually while passing us as though that ensured he had the right of way. Being an alert driver took on a whole new meaning in Nigeria! I did not have any desire to drive in this country. And everyone wished I would stop being a backseat driver.

Phil had to negotiate driving all over the road to dodge as many potholes as possible. Some of them were so deep because of the rainy season that the whole car in front of us disappeared before coming up on the other side. *This is going to be a long trip! Phil will be exhausted because I'm not offering to drive.*

"*Huppa*! (Hausa expression for frustration) We're getting blocked in again," Phil complained, slowing our vehicle down to a crawl. We were in another "go slow traffic jam." Two drivers behind us pulled out and drove up beside the car in front of us. They probably wanted to get a better view of what was causing the traffic jam. Soon there were five vehicles side by side all wanting to move forward and vehicles lined side by side facing us from the other direction as well.

"It will take more time to unravel this mess of vehicles than what caused the slow traffic in the first place!" I declared.

Finally arriving in Jos after thirteen hours of travel, we stayed together in Phil's renovated second-floor dorm room designated for teachers' living quarters. The large open area served as a combined kitchenette, living room, and bedroom with one set of bunk beds.

I had to starve Rene for twelve hours in preparation for the x-ray tests the doctor ordered. My heart ached when she screamed in hunger and frustration. I wanted my newborn to learn to trust me to meet her needs when she cried.

The next day I waited in the hospital watching the commotion in front of me while bouncing my fussy newborn. Finally, the expatriate surgeon came to meet me.

"Good morning. I'm sorry, but the x-ray technician didn't show up for work today." *You've got to be kidding me! Of all the days for the x-ray technician to not show up for work! Why today? Why my baby?*

The surgeon continued, "I don't want to ask you to go through another twelve hours of not being able to feed your newborn again."

"Yeah, it was torture for us both," I agreed.

"Would you trust me to take the pictures?" He asked, without offering any other option.

"I guess so. Whatever you think is best," I replied impulsively, bouncing Rene in my arms.

Rene drank the bottle of chalky liquid for the x-rays without any complaints. I waited for the x-ray results outside the building, away from the chaos.

When the surgeon returned, he said, "Unfortunately I couldn't make any conclusions from the twelve pictures since I didn't use enough radiation. I apologize. The test can't be repeated because of the risk of too much radiation for Rene's health." *I just put Rene through twelve hours of no milk and then exposed her to x-rays for nothing. And I still know nothing about the source of the blood. I'm beyond frustrated!* I ended the conversation and left quickly because Rene was desperate to nurse. Tears flowed down my face and clouded my vision as I traveled back to Phil's dorm room.

Two days later, Rene broke out in a bright red rash on her face, arms, and hands. The only pediatrician in Jos agreed to examine her. After an assessment, he said, "Rene has an enlarged liver. Possibly a liver parasite or fluke (worm) crossed the placenta while she was in utero. A fluke could cause the spitting up of blood clots," he continued, "but I'm hoping that it has worked its way out of her system." Rene hadn't been gaining weight, which the doctor attributed to a fluke as well.

I was ecstatic to finally hear a possible diagnosis and was eager to share with Darrel what the pediatrician concluded. After holding my breath for so long, I could finally breathe deeply once again.

*****

Breath

"Phil, would you be willing to take care of Obe and Rene so I can take a bath?" I asked.

"Sure thing," Phil replied without hesitation. Phil was always willing to help in whatever way he could. Obe crawled up on his lap with a book.

I secured Rene in a flimsy infant seat given to us as a baby gift. While in the bathtub, I heard her cry but was satisfied that Phil could take care of her needs.

"Sherill, Rene turned blue!" Phil screamed.

"Bring her here!" I ordered as I jumped out of the bathtub, flinging the door wide open.

He passed my limp, blue baby to me. Instantly, I began doing mouth-to-mouth respirations until Rene started to breathe again within seconds. My stark-naked dripping body shook uncontrollably while I held Rene close to my chest.

After I comforted Rene and got dressed, I asked Phil what had happened. He explained that though he tried to soothe Rene, she became more upset, arched her back, and suddenly pitched herself forward. She hit her head on the cement floor facedown with the infant seat strapped on her back. I assumed she had a seizure caused by her head hitting the concrete.

That night I wrestled with God and myself. *Am I capable of keeping my children safe? What kind of mother am I to take risks that leave my children in crises? I barely have time to process one event before something else happens. And where is God in all of this? We have committed ourselves to following a sense of call to go overseas for at least three years to partner with Nigerians in ministry. Doesn't God have some obligation to show up in these types of situations? How do we recover from medical crises with our children, being terminated by our supervisor, and having no place to live all in less than a year? I could have never imagined our present reality in my wildest dreams!*

My trust in God was unraveling, and I couldn't stop the process. . .

3

Liminal Journey with Obe's Life-threatening Illness

THE RHYTHMIC SOUND OF the whirring fan propped on a stool blocks out my ruminating thoughts of our past year in Nigeria and the medical crises with Rene, enticing me to doze. I jerk myself awake momentarily and look at Obe. I cannot sleep now! The life of my son depends on my being alert.

My nurse brain checks off the list - his chest is rising rhythmically, the IV is still rapidly dripping, his IV site has no signs of infiltration, he does not feel feverish, and he has not vomited or had diarrhea in the last six hours. But his diaper is not even damp. How long will it take for the IV fluids to get his kidneys working again? Days of continuous vomiting, diarrhea, and fever have stressed his small body to the maximum.

Why, oh why, do I think that my being trained as a nurse will enable me to protect my children in a rural area without the health resources I am used to? I know enough to recognize all the things that can happen but feel helpless to prevent them.

As the night shadows envelope me, matching the darkness within, a deep loneliness fills my soul. Even God is distant; I cannot pray. My eyes have no tears left.

I hear Darrel's alarm ringing. He will take a shift to give me a break to hopefully get some sleep. Darrel gives me a long hug and rubs my shoulders and neck muscles to relieve the tension. After sitting at Obe's side a few minutes, he suggests we pray together once again for the life of our son.

"God, we feel so out of control!" Darrel prays. "And we feel so alone, not knowing how to even pray." Through his sobs, with his face in his hands, he haltingly continues, "You have given us our son as a gift, please protect his life! We beg you to touch his body and heal him! And we stand against the powers of darkness in Jesus's name if in any way there is a spiritual battle going on in this place."

No longer trusting the effectiveness of our own prayers, I beg, "Jesus, please speak to someone in the United States to pray with us for the life of our son!"

Rene's cries from her makeshift bed of an open footlocker interrupt our prayer. I quickly go to pick her up, so she doesn't waken Obe. There is no baby bed to be found in this area. I can't even find baby clothes.

What little baby supplies I had obtained, I stored in a chest of drawers and mice had eaten holes in them. My sister had mailed us Gerber plastic diaper covers, but the envelope had been sliced open and all but one had been stolen. Before flying to Nigeria, my mother-in-law criticized me for "wanting to take all of America" to Nigeria. Apparently, I was not as spiritual as my husband or his family to trust God for all these things. In my effort to prove that I was trusting God to provide, my resolve melted away. I left behind the car seats and other baby supplies so I would not appear to be a wealthy American living in Nigeria. I now call it irresponsibility! Why not bring car seats for our children with the crazy driving in Nigeria? And with all that has been happening to us, I do not know what "trust in God" even means anymore.

Eight-week-old Rene places her tiny hand on my breast as I nestle her into position and help her attach securely to nurse. Later, I gaze at my blissfully satiated baby in my arms. Gratitude surges through my veins for her health. Simultaneously, I remind myself again of the total dependency of my newborn and almost two-year-old on our decisions in medical crises and feel the heavy responsibility. I carefully lay Rene inside the padded footlocker and return to check on Obe. He is still sleeping peacefully, and his diaper seems a bit damp. *Or am I imagining it?* With a sigh of relief, I wonder if I dare to believe he will come through this and recover.

I've been hearing a gnawing noise at the kitchen door for the last hour. Darrel checks it out. A rat is chewing on the bottom of the door. Darrel grabs a broom and chases it away. But the rat keeps returning. He finally places a small lamp right at the door and the rat decides to meander on to other night activities.

"This must be the rat that keeps eating holes in our papayas each night," I say. "Darrel, you can't sleep while Obe is so weak. He may not even cry if the rat gets near enough to bite him."

Later, after what feels like only minutes, Darrel gently pats my shoulder to waken me. He tells me that the IV of 800 milliliters is finished, so I unhook the IV and place Obe in his bed. Darrel and I drop exhausted into our own bed. Obe's cry wakens us two hours later. His diarrhea has soaked through double terry cloth diapers, his blanket, and the bed. The battle rages on. *I doubt the person who stole the rubber diaper covers needs them as much as I do now.*

The doctor arrives for a house call in the morning. We explain to him that we have not been successful in convincing Obe to drink anything. The doctor is alarmed and orders an additional 2,400 milliliters of IV fluid. I continue to run IV's into Obe's veins over the next few days while Rene presents with head congestion and a cough, making it more difficult for her to nurse. Darrel assures me that the teachers at the school are thinking and praying for both Obe and Rene. The neighbors nearby also share their concern for our children.

As I care for my two sick little ones, my thoughts are focused on the task ahead. *How are we going to accomplish moving soon? I can't imagine finding the physical energy to pack everything up again.* We must move out of this temporary house near the clinic because the owner needs it for an employee. He has already given us an extension of a month, so there are no options for further negotiations. There is also a shortage of gasoline in the country, adding uncertainty to our plans for moving. We have not yet found a place to move to since hearing of the termination of our assignment. Are we returning to the United States, moving to northern Nigeria to join a similar agency, or staying here longer? Without further clarity, it feels almost impossible to discern what to do.

Obe slowly regains strength. We celebrate each step along the way: Obe eating two crackers and keeping it down, Obe drinking a half glass of water in a morning, etc. The day he is well enough to get out of bed and dress, his elastic-waist shorts fall to the floor because he has lost so much weight.

Obe's second August birthday arrives. He is still refusing many foods. Our Lutheran expatriate friend, who lives a two-hour drive away, bakes and decorates a train cake for Obe. He barely tastes it, but the rest of us celebrate the milestone of Obe turning two with eating and dancing.

Letters take three weeks to arrive from the United States. One day a letter arrives from a friend in Virginia. Our friend's four-year-old daughter, Tamara, loves Obe. *She often sat behind us in church in Virginia. We could hear her saying, "Obe Darrel, Obe Darrel, Obe Darrel" because she liked to repeat his name. Her mother had written to us earlier that Tamera prays every night for Obe.*

In this letter her mother wrote that one night Tamara changed her prayer, "God, please make Obe well."

"We didn't hear that Obe is sick," her mother explained to Tamara, but for five nights in a row, the four-year-old continued to pray for Jesus to make Obe well.

In checking the dates from the letter, this four-year-old listened to God's whisper and stood in the gap with us with her prayers during the first excruciating days when Obe's dehydration was a threat to his life. Out of the mouth of babes!

God does care! I am so grateful!

*****

Mission Delegation Visit

Though we have been terminated from our assignment, we are required to wait until a mission agency delegation comes for a visit before moving to the north for another assignment or returning to the United States. In the meantime, we do not know how to make wise decisions. We eventually sell our furniture and take a vacation in Jos in northern Nigeria while we wait.

In anticipation of the arrival of the delegation, we travel the five-hundred miles south and stay in a guesthouse where we can host the delegation. Our Lutheran expatriate friends surprise us the evening before the delegation's arrival with a bottle of wine and a homemade rhubarb crunch. In a toast with wine, they share words of affirmation with us, stating their perceptions of our strength of character and resilience in difficult circumstances. We drink in their words as well as their wine. The most meaningful communion experience ever! What an expression of love!

The delegation arrives on our sixth wedding anniversary, two months after our termination. Our supervisor does not come because of "family concerns." One man on the delegation is a previous missionary with the agency who had left West Africa years earlier because of emotional struggles. Another couple on the delegation has served in Ghana with our mission agency.

On arrival at the guesthouse, the wife asks, "So why are you living in a guesthouse rather than your own place?"

My heart sinks to my ankles! *Don't they even know that we have been waiting for a delegation to come for almost five months? This must mean that the agency didn't orient the delegation to our situation. What are they thinking?* Hope suddenly disappears like a fleeting wind.

Meetings with the delegation and the Nigerian Church occur every day for a week, and Darrel is the driver. I cook dinner for the delegation while caring for our children and washing clothes by hand. Every evening they gather in private meetings, out of our earshot, to discuss our situation. We are not invited to join them.

"Darrel, we obviously are not really part of this agency. We are not part of the team! We are only their driver and cook!" I declare.

"I'm sorry, honey. What have we been waiting for in these five months if this is what we get? I never dreamed we would be talked *about* rather than *listened to* and included in decision-making."

We openly speak with the delegation about the unintentional struggles present in our relationship with the principal. *Before we could settle in a house in the beginning of our time in Nigeria, we had needed cash, but the Nigerian bank said it would take weeks for a United States check to be processed. The principal had accompanied us to the Nigerian bank and knew we needed Nigerian money for purchasing supplies. He gave us the proper Nigerian amount in local currency after we wrote him a personal check. A few months later, we received the returned check. We noticed it had not been cashed in Nigeria, but rather in Holland. Our mission colleagues explained that if the Nigerian authorities discovered our check being sold on the black market, they would revoke our visa and force us to leave the country. We suspected that someone in the Nigerian bank had sold our check on the black market to double the amount. In sharing our assumption with the principal, we were surprised to learn that he was the one who had sold our check on the black market. The principal offered us half of his profit, but we declined. Didn't he know that this could jeopardize our being here in Nigeria? Honesty in this culture is defined differently than what we're used to in our culture, that's for sure. Apparently, bribes and using the black market are norms for this country.*

In an evening meeting with the delegation at the guesthouse, Darrel explains, "I was told the mission agency does not financially support secondary schools. The school here in Nigeria is clearly a financially struggling secondary school rather than a seminary, and the mission agency continues to send monthly checks to support the operational costs of the school. I was told earlier that the mission agency has wired $25,000 annually for the last four years to the principal for the running of the school."

He continues, "The principal is often not present at the school, so I hear the discontent and anger of the teachers. Though the principal says there is no money to pay the teachers, he appeared recently at the school with his brand-new Peugeot vehicle. I have tried to discuss some of the problems with the principal, though I probably didn't always raise the issues in a culturally appropriate manner. As the Vice Principal, I've asked how I can be helpful, but it only seems to threaten the relationship further."

Darrel sighs and is silent before continuing to acknowledge his own mistakes. "I learned only after several months of teaching that my wearing shorts to school in the extreme heat does not culturally align with my higher position as vice principal. I have been open in my relationship with the other teachers as well. I believe my choice of dress and listening to the teachers has likely fed the principal's distrust of me as he maintains distance in relationship with the teachers."

"That's very cultural," the wife on the delegation says. "So how is teaching for you?"

"I never know whether I will even teach on any given day. The teachers aren't motivated when they aren't being paid for up to five months at a time. Students are failing their courses. Many days the principal instructs the teachers and me to supervise the students doing farm work, cutting the grass, or playing sports. Other days the students are sent home because school fees aren't paid," Darrel says with a flat tone, propping his elbows on his knees and his head on his hands. "I don't know how much longer I can maintain this role."

"I'm sorry that so many difficult things have happened to you that only add to your discouragement in this assignment," one of the men on the delegation says.

We are expecting the delegation to be a third party to help mediate in our situation, which would be culturally appropriate. Instead, they take Darrel by surprise in a church-wide meeting.

"Darrel, could you please explain what your struggle with the principal involves?" the head of the delegation asks. Darrel's mouth opens, but no words come out. He stares with bulging eyes at the man who asked the question.

What is he doing by setting Darrel up like this? The principal is a Nigerian church leader. Anything Darrel may say would shame the principal. Saving face is important in this culture. We made some mistakes previously as we were learning the culture, and we don't want to make more cultural mistakes now.

Everyone waits in silence. My stomach has flipped inside out. What can Darrel possibly say? He has good relationships with the teachers at the school and with many church pastors and lay leaders. And he has continued to work at building a better relationship with the principal despite all the circumstances.

"I don't know what to say," Darrel admits. He is sweating profusely and is looking at the ground.

Everyone continues to wait. He tries to choose his words carefully and to stick to speaking only of our experience without casting blame. There is no discussion after his statements. Darrel's face is downcast, avoiding eye contact, his shoulders slumped forward. *How I wish he had been included in the planning for this meeting. He would have never agreed to speak under these conditions. This almost makes it impossible for us to stay now.*

Back at the guesthouse, the delegation says that we appear to be "psychologically burned out," but we can stay in our assignment if we desire. Not only is this incredibly painful, but also confusing, since we've already been terminated by the agency months ago. And, in response, we have sold our furniture and have no place to live.

My sense of loneliness, abandonment, and lack of security leave me questioning God and myself. I feel caught in conflict with our housing and Darrel's employment at the school; I feel powerless to solve it. The conflict triggers deep pain in me from my childhood. Now, to hear we are "psychologically burned out" is filtered as "failure" to me. *Where is God in all this mess? And what does this "call of God" really mean anyway? Was God the one directing our steps to come to Nigeria?*

Darrel and I aren't sure how to process this feedback, that we are "psychologically burned out." Yes, we have had many crises in a short period of time, and it has been highly stressful. We have held on to hope in the delegation assisting us in our situation so we could continue to be involved with this church in Nigeria. The loss and grief in those expectations being shattered blinds us from finding renewed hope.

In the privacy of our bedroom, Darrel asks, "What about all the preparations we have done to be involved in missions? When I think about how long we've planned to serve in missions, even before we were married, it's hard for me to let go. We're not quitters."

"Yes," I say, "but you aren't enjoying your teaching anymore. You've begun to lose your motivation, just like the rest of the teachers. I don't view your years of training in Scotland as meaning we have to stay here in this situation."

"You're right. I guess we need to decide and risk the unknowns of the future again."

Darrel and I report our decision to the delegation the next morning at breakfast. "Sherill and I aren't prepared to remain in this assignment without more mediation," Darrel says in a monotone, his chin trembling.

In the combined church session that day, the leader of the delegation informs the local church leaders that although we are leaving to return to the United States, they will send another couple as soon as possible. *What does that say about us then? They view us as the ones with the problems.*

Back in our room later that evening, we both let out a long sigh and retreat inward to our separate worlds of thoughts and emotions. *Why had a delegation come? To diagnose us as psychologically unfit? And yet our mission friends on the ground see us as resilient. Instead of being supportive, we perceive the delegation's input as betrayal. I am relieved to be leaving Nigeria, but not in these circumstances. I have been determined to keep trying to build relationships and make the situation better, but I don't see a way forward. We're just not good enough mission workers to continue here.*

4

Returning to the United States

As part of our closure, we intentionally meet with friends like our language tutor, Udoffa and his wife, Akon, to say goodbye. Many people in the Nigerian church express disappointment in our leaving. We receive their thanks and take to heart their invitation to return.

After only fifteen months in Nigeria, we embark on the long journey back to the United States. I have malaria with fever and fatigue but travel anyway because our flights are scheduled. At this point, I desire to get on the plane and sleep. We fly into the airport in Brussels, Belgium, returning to the same gate we flew out of when leaving the United States. The diarrhea stain on the carpet from Obe's illness still marks our first visit to the airport.

The airline gives us a voucher for one night in a hotel in Brussels as a free benefit. We flag a taxi driver for a ride to our hotel.

After riding in the taxi for fifteen minutes, I am suspicious. "Darrel, why would the airline put us up in a hotel that is so far from the airport?" I ask.

"I don't know," Darrel says. "It does seem strange as we've passed other hotels."

On arrival at the hotel, we unload all our luggage on the sidewalk, along with our two little ones. Darrel hands the taxi driver the voucher for the ride. The driver rubs the voucher on his backside. With a flurry of arm movements, he mimes tearing it in two. He rubs his index finger and thumb together, indicating that he wants cash rather than the voucher. But we don't have any cash. Darrel tries to communicate our predicament with hand motions and English words. The taxi driver turns quickly, throwing one of our largest suitcases into the taxi. He runs to the driver's door, hops in, and restarts the engine. *Oh no! What is he doing?* Darrel instantaneously jumps into the backseat and throws the voucher for the hotel out the window onto the sidewalk for me as they speed away. Luckily, I grab it before it blows away.

Standing alone on the curb with a five-month-old baby, a two-year-old, and our luggage, including heavy footlockers, is more than I can physically handle by myself. I want to sit down and cry.

Are you serious, God? Does this painful story never end? I feel so vulnerable. What an ending to fifteen months of feeling abandoned!

The cries of the children register in my brain. With Rene in my arms, I take Obe's hand and walk up the embankment to the front of the hotel, leaving almost all the luggage out on the sidewalk.

"Sir, please, I need assistance!" I yell to a porter as I enter the door, before reaching the front desk. My tired, sick appearance adds to my desperate request and produces an immediate response. Several employees stop their work and jump up to assist me in checking in, retrieving my luggage, and leading me to our designated hotel room. I lock the door of our room and debate what to do. The children are hungry, but I don't have the energy to cope with taking them downstairs to a restaurant. Exhausted, I lay down on the double bed with the children and read to them. I keep praying for Darrel to return.

Eventually Darrel knocks on our door. Obe jumps up and down in his excitement to see Daddy back. After hugs, Darrel explains what happened. "The taxi driver returned me to the airport. This time it only took five minutes rather than twenty minutes. Then he proceeded to argue with other taxi drivers over the validity of our voucher. Another taxi driver finally decided to drive me back here, and he took the airline voucher as payment."

Early the next morning, we continue our flight to the United States. There is snow covering the ground when we land, and we have no winter clothes or coats for the children or ourselves. Two women, sent by the mission agency, are at the airport to meet us, one being our previous pastor's wife from our church in Virginia. She somehow convinces the official to allow her to enter the customs area to hold Rene so we can easily move through the process. It is so comforting to see someone familiar.

Before driving far from the airport, the car sputters, belching rebellious noises. We are looking for a gas station when the engine dies, and the car slowly comes to a halt. Darrel volunteers to walk in the snow without a coat or boots to a nearby house to call the mission agency personnel, explaining our need to be rescued from the cold. He comes back to join us.

We wait and wait in the car, trying to keep our children warm by wrapping our arms around them.

God, are you done testing us? We are back in the United States now. Or is waiting our indefinite spiritual discipline?

After waiting an hour in the cold car, Darrel trudges back to the house and makes a second phone call, only to discover that a person is trying to find us on the wrong road. Finally, a police officer stops to check on us. The police officer loads our luggage into the trunk of his car and gives our family a ride to the county line where he arranges for another police officer to transport us to the agency guesthouse. The two women will wait for the person from the agency.

Because of the time change, the little ones wake up at 3:00 a.m. the first night and don't go back to sleep. So, of course, Darrel and I can't either. In the morning, we meet with a group of mission agency staff. We sit across from eight men and one woman to tell our story as part of the planned debriefing.

"You have shared a deeply painful story of your experiences in Nigeria. How can you share it without any emotion?" one man asks at the end of our relating the story.

Because it's not safe for us to do so, that's why! After fifteen months of trying to be heard, we will wait for people we trust to help us debrief further.

I don't acknowledge my feelings though. "Yes, it has been deeply painful, but since many months have passed, much of our story is not as fresh anymore."

Two days later, we fly on to Virginia. But, once again we are homeless. We have had no time to talk with others to prepare for our return. Our friends, Elam and Harriet Steiner, graciously open their basement to us since it has a kitchenette and two bedrooms.

It is so good to have come full circle back home, to the beautiful mountainous Shenandoah Valley! Finally, I will find safe friends to help me process as we have more to unpack than just our clothes. We have significant trauma and emotional baggage to unpack as well. . .

5

Facing Emotional and Spiritual Pain and Brokenness

THOUGH WE RETURNED TO the United States, our experiences in Nigeria dominate our thoughts and emotions. Processing what happened to us in those fifteen months can't be shelved for a later time. We view ourselves as casualties. Our self-esteem has plummeted since we expected to live in Nigeria for ten years. How will we explain our experience when others ask questions?

We sink even lower when we read the delegation's report. They state that the mission agency needs to improve their screening process of applicants, questioning our sense of call to be in mission work. The report infers the agency needs to screen marriages more carefully, indirectly critiquing our marriage. To gain further understanding, I contact the woman on the delegation, who seemed to be the scribe for the team. In her response, she asserts that Darrel is a dominating husband. Her stated reasons are false. She must have misinterpreted what we shared. We read the response about our marriage to my mother-in-law, and she laughs too heartily. She knows I am perfectly capable of speaking up for myself in my marriage. Months later the mission agency makes a statement in their newsletter saying they take responsibility for the ending of our assignment. While we appreciate the statement, it doesn't go far enough. We would appreciate the mission agency requesting forgiveness for what we perceive as negligence in preparation for our time in Nigeria.

Our Nigerian experiences have broken apart my theology of God. If God did call us to go to Nigeria, what went wrong? Are we to blame? If God is in control of our lives, is all that we experienced God's will? What meaning does all the suffering have? There doesn't seem to be any redemptive purpose. If everything that happens to us is God's will, how do I view innocent children suffering physical or emotional pain? I've listened to victims of rape and abuse. Are their experiences part of God's will? If so, what kind of God is this, a sadistic one?

Our experiences in Nigeria and the resulting questions open my eyes to inner pain I have stuffed for years. It is now pushing to the surface. . .

*****

A few months after our return to the United States, we drive seventeen hours from Virginia to Florida to visit my parents and siblings. We arrive at my sister Miriam's home and sit down to eat a celebratory meal after two years of being separated from one another. Dad, in his usual jovial manner, shares his latest jokes with us. My brother Dave, the oldest, who lives four hours away, is present, along with his family. He updates us on their lives.

When there is a bit of silence, Mother enters the conversation. "Darrel, we have heard that you are to speak at our church on Sunday. What makes you so special that they invited you to be the preacher?" Mother asks.

"I don't know," Darrel says. "Maybe you'll have to ask them."

Mother continues with her unwelcoming disparaging comments. "Darrel, you look like you've gained weight. Have you gained a lot since returning from Africa? I think . . ."

My brother, Dave, interrupts, "You know, Mother, with comments like that, who needs enemies?"

My sister, Miriam, stands up and immediately asks, "Who would like more chicken?" She knows Mother is critical of all of us. We have learned it is best to change the subject.

*****

A few days later, during the two-mile drive to Mother and Dad's house, Rene falls asleep. She desperately needs a good nap for our sanity as well as hers. I call ahead to request that Mother prepare a place where I can lay Rene down; hopefully, she will remain asleep.

At their house, Darrel first checks in with Mother to see if a place is ready for Rene. I then carefully carry Rene into the bedroom, lay her down, and pat her back to ensure she will remain asleep.

Mother appears in the bedroom with hands on her hips and in a loud voice says, "I don't want that mattress to get urine on it. Pick her up so I can place a garbage bag underneath the sheet."

Rene opens her eyes, picks up her head, and looks around the room. All my work to help her stay asleep is wasted.

"Mother, I called ahead so you could prepare where you wanted me to lay her down. Now that she's had a cat nap in the car, and is awake, she will not go back to sleep. You've accomplished exactly what I was trying to prevent!" My chest feels tight as I pick up Rene in defeat.

Later, Dad asks me if I know why Mother is upset. I explain what happened, and Dad says he understands.

That evening in the foyer, when saying goodbye for the last time on this trip, I lean over to hug Mother. I may as well be hugging a cold statue. Her parsed set lips, blazing eyes, and arms resolutely remaining at her side speak volumes. I express my thanks for the dinner and say they are welcome to come to Virginia and visit us. Uncomfortable silence permeates the air.

"I. wish. you. had. never. come," Mother says, spitting out the words slowly while not moving a muscle.

Chills flow down my spine. My body shakes uncontrollably as tears blur the sight of her. I quickly hug Dad and walk out the door.

Darrel calls back later and asks permission to stop over the next morning on our way out of town to pick up Obe's stuffed monkey mistakenly left at their house. Dad agrees. On arrival, I find the monkey outside on the porch. I hear Mother walking around inside. *Maybe she has calmed down and we can hug goodbye this morning.* I ring the doorbell and wait. No one comes. I ring the doorbell again. No one comes. I conclude this is most likely intentional on her part, so we leave for home.

On the trip back to Virginia, the deep pain of rejection is all too familiar, both from my childhood and from our experience in Nigeria. I can no longer shut the lid on the pain I have stuffed. It is time to process memories from the past. . .

*****

I Am Not Enough!

Flashes of memories come back to me from my childhood. They are often fraught with Mother's complicated personality. I sometimes don't understand her responses to me, even if I have tried hard to please her.

*****

"Hold still, Sherill!" Mother says. "I can't create your curls if you keep squirming."

"I wish I could go to church without curls," I say standing tall and crossing my arms across my chest.

"Everyone thinks you two look so cute with your curls," Mother says, using the comb to part another section of hair.

I'm seven years old and my sister, Miriam, is eight and a half. Since being toddlers, Mother has insisted on curling our hair for church. Mother uses some clear gooey stuff on our hair to form eight long vertical curls hanging around our heads. She wraps our wet, sticky hair tightly around her finger, using a blow dryer to dry the curls. Then she carefully pulls her finger out. People keep telling Mother how cute we are in matching, homemade, yellow-and white dresses with our long curls. Mother's face lights up with a big smile, and she thanks them for their compliments.

I like to play and run around with my friends at church, but Mother gets upset that my hair gets messy, and my curls fall out. Who cares about curls?

David, Miriam, and Sherill

Although we don't like the curls, we do love the dresses Mother sews for us. Clothes in the stores cost too much. My aunt says Mother sews clothes like a professional seamstress.

Mother hides in a locked bedroom for days before Christmas. We don't know what she is doing. On Christmas Day, we open our presents. We find clothes she has sewn for our dolls. Some of the doll clothes match our dresses. They are beautiful! Such tiny lace around the sleeves and hem. We think our doll clothes are prettier than the ones we could buy in the store.

I wish we had more money, though, as Mother says there is too much work to do at home in caring for our family. *When David was three and Miriam was born, Mother had a live-in nanny who helped with the work. Before I was born, Mother and Dad moved from Michigan to Ohio, and there was no money for a nanny.*

Mother gets tired. We help as much as we can. On Sunday mornings, I sometimes tell Mother, "If you're too busy, you can stop making curls for us."

"We need to look our best for church," Mother replies.

*****

One day, I tell Mother that my friend Kathy's little brother is being potty trained. And he's two and a half. "Are you sure you potty trained me when I was six-months-old," I ask.

"I just knew how to do it," Mother says. "I tied you and Miriam to your potty chairs after you ate and waited, and you'd go potty eventually!"

"One time I lost Miriam and couldn't find her," Mother chuckles in remembering the story. "I looked everywhere for her, even walking outside in case she wandered off. I panicked because I couldn't find her anywhere. Finally, I discovered Miriam had fallen asleep tied to her potty chair. I forgot and left her there, so she just took a nap." Mother says.

*****

I find Mother in her favorite glider chair with her feet up on the footstool. *We are living in Florida in a small house Dad had built. Dad had moved to Florida ahead of us to find carpentry work.*

I hand her my report card from the first quarter of fourth grade. We read the report together, while I lean over the back of her chair.

Turning her head to face me, Mother says, "Why do you have a 'C' on your report card? This is the first 'C' you have received. What are you going to do to turn that into an 'A'?"

"I don't know," I mumble under my breath as I run out of the room before she sees the tears forming in my eyes. I find a place where I can hide in the garage among all the boxes of extra things Mother has collected.

I have seven "A's" on this report card. Why doesn't she have anything to say about those? And why doesn't she wonder about the teacher giving me a "C" in writing? Last year my third-grade teacher had posted my handwritten papers on the bulletin board as examples of good writing. So why does this teacher not like my handwriting this year? I don't understand the teachers or my mother. I'm just not good enough.

*****

Wow, this sermon is scary! The preacher is describing hell in a booming, deep voice. I glance at Mother and Dad, and they don't look scared. I guess they already know all about hell. I don't want to die and go to hell. Though I'm only nine years old, I know children die sometimes.

Our family has been attending these revival tent meetings each evening this week. The sermons all scare me. When I hear an invitation to become a Christian so you can go to Heaven, I stand to my feet and walk down the sawdust covered aisle. A counselor talks with me and explains the words I can use to pray. Then I ask Jesus to forgive me and become my Savior.

I rejoin Mother, and she asks,. "Sherill, do you understand what it means to become a Christian? Or do you only want to wear the prayer veil?" In our church, women who are baptized wear a white cloth prayer veil, made of delicate netting material, to show their submission to God, their husbands, and the church leaders (I Corinthians 11:13).

"No, Mother, I don't even want to wear it!" *Mother thinks I am not serious about the commitment I just made, but I am nine years old! I thought this would at least please her!*

I guess this means our pastor will baptize me in front of the whole church now. I hope he doesn't pour lots of water on my head. My hair will look dreadful afterwards.

*****

I rub the smudge on the sliding glass door with more umph. I still need to clean out the refrigerator. Mother says I can wait to clean the oven until next week. Miriam and I must do the weekly cleaning and laundry on Saturdays before we can do anything with friends. Sometimes we miss out on fun invitations. We promise to do our chores later, but Mother says work comes before play.

Mother comes to inspect my window washing. Without thinking I blurt out, "Why am I to wash the windows, mow the lawn, hang up the clothes, scrub the oven, and clean out the refrigerator? Miriam only dusts and vacuums and cooks, but she isn't doing any of this hard work! And she's older! She didn't do this work when she was nine."

"Your sister is frail and nutritionally deficient. You are strong and muscular and can do these chores; she can't," Mother explains.

I can't see anything weak or frail about Miriam. When Miriam and I have wet washcloth fights, she stings my skin like a pro. She is smaller than I am, and Mother says I am "stockier," whatever that means. I think I must be adopted. Miriam must be the "real" daughter. She is treated so differently. I think I am an "Orphan Annie" in this house. At least Annie understands me.

*****

"Sherill's tongue color shows that she needs more Vitamin A," the nutritionist says to Mother.

Mother believes I need to see the nutritionist as well as Miriam now. And it always results in more pills to swallow. *Maybe we could save money by not eating food; we could just take our pills and go to school! What an awful idea!*

We are also required to eat yucky food. Mother makes us eat plain sour yogurt before we can eat anything else for supper. Before I go out to mow the yard, Mother forces me to eat a heaping tablespoon of horseradish. I gag and almost vomit. Mother says it "cleans out my sinuses." She makes homemade tonics by the gallon and stores them in an extra refrigerator in our garage. Mother forces us to drink a glass of tonic before supper. I hold my nose tightly shut because the smell is as bad as the taste.

I love spending time at my friends' houses. They eat tasty food without being forced to drink tonics and eat sour yogurt. I like it better at my friends' houses anyway. Marilyn's and Kathy's mothers are nice and don't yell at us if we want more than one apple.

When I do get sick, Mother doesn't take me to a doctor. She takes me to a neighbor who has a machine that "checks us out for what ails us." He places my hand over a shiny metal ball within the machine and moves it around. After he gets clues of what is wrong with me, he tells me to stretch out my arms on each side. He places some pills in one hand and instructs me to focus on keeping my arm raised up; he then tries to push my arm down. If he is successful, it means the pills are not the correct solution for my sickness. Mother says this is "body muscle assessment." *I think our family believes in magic!*

Mother believes doctors will make you sicker. She views all vaccines as poison. When my school required proof of vaccinations to start school, she put up a fight with the principal. Mother won that battle.

*****

We all, including Dad, view Mother as the deeply spiritual person in the family. She prays the longest prayers and often has "words from God" for us that relate to our behavior. Our children's bedtime storybook tells stories about those who don't obey God and the bad things that may happen to them. A children's song from Sunday School keeps me in line. I am to be careful what my eyes see and what my ears hear, because there is a Father up above who is looking down on me. The end of the song says God is looking down in love, but I feel scared in knowing God is watching everything I do.

This is the picture of God in my mind, one who is looking down to watch and criticize whatever I do that isn't perfect. I try to make God proud of me. When I think about God, I hear Mother's corrective words, "Straighten up, Sherill! Obedience is the key to life! So, keep your eyes, ears, and mouth pure!"

6

Searching for God and Self-Identity as a Teenager

MY STOMACH GROWLS WHILE smelling the aroma of the chicken and veggies I am sautéing in the frying pan for supper. Mother comes in and scans the kitchen where I have been chopping and slicing veggies. Miriam and I are often required to cook the evening meals.

"You dropped broccoli and onion skins on the floor again, Sherill! You create such a mess. Why can't you be more careful?" Mother says in a condescending tone, flailing her right arm in a sweeping motion over the entire area.

"Sorry! I'm in a hurry since I have homework to finish. If you can do it better, then I'm happy to let you cook!" I retort as I continue stirring the veggies in the pan.

Whack! My right jaw stings from the harsh sudden slap across my face, whipping my neck to my left side. My mind spins, trying to comprehend the surprising force of the slap that I didn't see coming from behind me. The combination of my eyes stinging from the onions and the humiliation of what just happened overwhelm my urge to hide my vulnerability. Tears drip down onto my shirt as shame rises within me.

"Don't you disrespect me! You know better!" Mother exclaims, stomping off to her bedroom.

I find it difficult to keep my mouth shut and end up talking back to Mother, but it never goes well. I struggle to control my emotions, and I'm disrespectful at times. Sometimes Mother seems to be in a state of rage. One day she overpowers me and pins my arms flush to the wall, while she screams at me with blazing eyes. I'm afraid of her rage because I don't know when it may erupt or what she may do.

God, is there anyone that can help our family? Everyone thinks we are a loving Christian family. That seems more like a dream than reality.

*****

One day Mother is exceptionally angry with my brother, Dave. She directs Dad to chase Dave around the bedroom, whipping him with a black belt, even though he's now sixteen years old. Mother blocks the locked door so he can't get away. She screams both her demands to Dad and her accusations of my brother.

Mother has sort of disowned Dave. She no longer irons his dress shirts or assists him in any way. My brother tells me that Mother claims she got pregnant with him from the Devil. I try to be the peacemaker in the family. Even though he punches me with his knuckles in my upper arm when he passes me in the house, I iron Dave's shirts and clean his room.

When my father succeeds in whipping Dave with the belt, all I can hear anywhere in the house is my mother screaming and my brother yelping. I don't want to listen anymore! I walk out of the house without a flashlight into the night and roam aimlessly in the streets.

Why is Mother angry much of the time? Everything in the family centers around trying to keep her calm and happy. No matter how I try to please her, it's hopeless to dream she will be satisfied with me. My hair is messy, my thighs are fat, I weigh too much, I'm not respectful enough, I don't jump up fast enough when she wants something, it costs too much money to raise me. I am just not enough!

*****

While spending time at my friends' houses, I observe their mothers interacting with them, giving them compliments, thanking them, and hugging them. My dream is to have a loving relationship with my own mother. I don't invite my friends over very often because I never know which side of my mother I will find. She may be nice and friendly, or she may be in her own world, ignoring us until we irritate her in some way. It usually isn't worth the risk.

When we ask permission to do something or go somewhere, Mother frequently says no. So, what's the solution? Stop asking. We now give our parents vague, partially true ideas of where we're going. Before going roller skating or to a movie with our friends, we hide clothes under our jackets and change into them in the car in the church parking lot.

By age thirteen, I'm dating a twenty-one-year-old guy who assumes I am sixteen. I am smitten with his attention. It is the beginning of dating many older guys. I seek their acceptance, affection, and love. Coming home from a date, though, I often cry because the guys aren't dating me for who I really am; they just want to make out and fondle me. The hole in my soul is so deep. And dating isn't filling it.

*****

My mother finds me paid cleaning jobs when I turn twelve. Then as a teenager, I work as a salesclerk at the Belk Lindsey's store in the evenings and on weekends. I'm earning money to be able to buy my own clothes and have a bit of spending money. This beats cleaning for other families!

Often when I bring home a new shirt from a store, Mother will ask why I haven't brought an identical one for her. Mother loves to shop for clothes now. Appearance matters greatly. She is petite and often buys junior girls size clothes for her slight frame. It doesn't matter to her that a peasant style dress isn't stylish or appropriate for her age. She buys clothes on clearance and decides she will alter them if they don't fit quite right. Often, after pinning the alteration, she doesn't follow through with the sewing. It's always more fun to go shopping again.

Mother and Dad are selling electric boards that are placed under mattresses. The theory is that it will align all the electricity in your body and heal you from whatever is out of balance. They require us to pay for these boards for our beds. Miriam and I strongly react to this idea. But we give in to Mother's insistence. Sometimes it's easier to do whatever Mother wants than to deal with the ongoing battle.

Dad is deeply involved in his work as a fine trim carpenter and is known as an excellent craftsman in his trade. He also spends a lot of time singing in groups and leading worship in church or teaching classes. His identity and affirmation come from outside the home, and this probably helps him cope with Mother's frequent criticisms of him. Dad has the uncanny ability to push the negative out of his mind and focus on "worshipping the Lord."

*****

Late Teens

The walls of our house are gradually closing in on me inside an environment of anger, criticism, and control. My world, rather than expanding, is gradually shrinking like a moving fence closing in at night on a thoroughbred horse who desires to gallop, but the decreased space doesn't allow for that freedom. I desire to develop my skills, but I find the fences of control moving in ever tighter circles around me. The fences that were meant for protection earlier in my life now feel restrictive and inhibiting.

Miriam and I want to jump the fence and find some open space. She decides to attend one year of college in Virginia. If Miriam is leaving, then I want to leave as well. I inquire about attending Eastern Mennonite High School located near the college Miriam will attend. The school admission's director says I can live in a dormitory as an out-of-state student for my senior year of high school. My parents don't want me to go, but I adamantly argue my case. Maybe they think it's better that Miriam doesn't go alone. Whatever the reason, they decide to let us both go. We pay most of the expense from our saved income.

Off we ride to an adventure beyond the fence. . .

*****

Senior Year

Attending Eastern Mennonite High School for my senior year turns out to be a pivotal benchmark. It changes the trajectory of my life. I forge new friendships in the first weeks. In the dorm, I float around in a dreamlike state in the freedom and life-giving community of friends. The teachers at the school demonstrate that they care for their students in a way that I could have only dreamed possible. My acceptance into music groups becomes a natural place for me to belong and to excel in my identity as an excellent vocalist.

I am thrilled to be accepted into the school's touring choir. The choir director chooses me to sing an alto solo for a competition the choir participates in with other private schools. In preparation for the competition, he gives me voice lessons. I soak up all that he teaches me.

At the competition, I listen to other high school choirs singing for the judges and my pulse quickens. They sound so professional, and their enunciation is so clear. The responsibility of singing the acapella solo in our choir's song for the judges weighs heavily upon me.

Before it is our turn to sing for the judges, the choir director says, "Sherill, I've been informed that there won't be an extra microphone for your solo. You will need to project your voice to be heard well. You can do it!" he says. I will have to start the song by myself and sing the ending alone as well. *What if I open my mouth to sing and nothing comes out? Or what if I go sharp or flat?* They are all depending on me.

I roll my tongue around my gums and swallow hard. My mouth is so dry. I continue to sip from my water bottle. But if I drink too much, I may feel the urge to relieve myself. I don't know how long it will be before they call our school's name.

I hear the announcer call for our choir. I walk out to the front of the stage and take a deep breath, with a silent prayer to God for confidence. I open my mouth and begin singing "Kyrie, Eleison" meaning, "Lord, have mercy." Trying to forget about judges listening, I sing that prayer from the depths of my being.

The applause at the end is reassuring, but my heart is still beating so fast. When a judge moves to the microphone, I hold my breath, only to momentarily hear we have received the highest rating for our performance. What a relief! An ecstatic satisfaction washes over me as I bask in the joy of accomplishment.

*****

During the fall spiritual emphasis week at school, I recommit my life to God. I later share my testimony in chapel. That same day a handsome blond guy, Darrel, known by the girls to be "cool," asks me to go on a date. Unbelievable! I end up beating Darrel Hostetter in miniature golf that evening. That probably doesn't make a good impression. Following our date, Darrel hardly speaks to me, even to greet me in the halls at school. Confusing, to say the least. Much later, I hear that he thinks I seem shy and unhappy as a new student. I assume he feels released from his duty to care now.

Because I can't foresee a spiritually mature guy ever desiring to date me, I continue to gravitate toward the elusive acceptance and "love" from the "wild" college guys near the high school campus. While never meeting my gaze, one of the college girls, an acquaintance from Florida, tells me her story of dating the wrong type of guys in college. *She left college after getting pregnant. After giving the baby up for adoption, she then returned to college.* While she looks for a tissue to wipe her eyes, she warns me that the guys I am dating could take me down a similar path. I mull her words for a few weeks and finally stop dating the college guys.

I sit in front of Darrel in Math Analysis, and we talk quietly during class about our lives and our relationship with God. The teacher has a dual role as dorm "Mom," as well as teaching math. She allows Darrel and me to talk in class, even though she assumes I may not be able to do the homework without her help in the dorm. Her assumptions are correct. My grades in this class result in a drop in my grade point average. I am chosen as the salutatorian rather than the valedictorian of the class with only a two-hundredths of a point difference in our grade point average. But some things are of greater importance in life than grades.

Darrel speaks freely about his relationship with God, paving the way for me to be more vulnerable. Gradually I risk expressing my faith and struggles. Intimacy with God grows, and I find an assurance in truly being a part of the family of God.

Over the school year, Darrel spiritually mentors and supports me. He serves as a Christ figure for me by demonstrating God's unconditional love and care in ways I have never experienced before. Darrel's commitment to God challenges me. I love his passion for adventure. When I am with him, I relax. By the end of the year, we are officially dating. Darrel respects my mind and body and loves me for who I am as a person. The relationship matches my dreams.

*****

One date with Darrel, that does not cost him money, involves cave exploring. The Shenandoah Valley in Virginia has many known caves to explore. As we drive to the location, he excitedly describes the cave with a fifty-foot drop down to the bottom.

Darrel ties the rope to a stump on the ground near the opening of the cave. I then push off the rocks with my feet as I lower myself down into the cave while holding on to the rope. The dark, shadowy cave rooms exude an eeriness that I find uncomfortable. Mud and standing water greet me at the bottom of the cave. I don't complain, though, as I would do anything just to be with Darrel.

After examining the walls around us to determine how we might explore the cave further, we climb up the rocky wall of the cave to a small cleft where we can both stand. Then Darrel climbs higher up the side of the cleft. Suddenly his feet are sliding on the damp rock wall, and he struggles to find solid footing.

The side of the wall crumbles beneath his feet. "Oh no!" Darrel yells.

We're going to fall off into the crevice far below! We could both die in this cave! Instantly, I brace my feet against the sides of the ledge I am on and literally catch him in my arms, pressed smack together in the small space between the walls.

Neither of us speak at first. "Thank you," Darrel whispers in my ear. We climb the rope back out of the cave in silence.

On the ride home, I am lost in my own reflections.

"What are you deep in thought about?" Darrel asks.

"We could have been seriously injured in falling off the ledge to the cave floor below! And our flashlights could have dropped to the bottom of the canyon below in the process!"

"Sherill, I'm sorry. It probably isn't the safest cave to explore."

"You can say that again!"

"I know we need to be cautious. Remember, though, that adventure involves risks. You won't do much in life if you always think through all the possible risks before you try something. Look, you caught me. We're fine." Darrel says, turning to look my direction with a twinkle in his eye. *His words don't muster up confidence within me!*

Is this a sign of the future if I stay connected to this man? I admire his sense of adventure; however, I am more of a realist, and I'm not comfortable taking dangerous risks.

When we part ways after graduation, Darrel gifts me his enlarged senior picture. I cherish his photo and the heart of love and friendship symbolized by the gift.

Darrel's high school senior picture

Sherill's high school senior picture

*****

Following graduation, Darrel's parents and younger brothers moved to Nigeria, West Africa, for a three-year mission service term. Darrel moves from Virginia to Florida and lives with his aunt Peggy and uncle Michael across the street from our house. Uncle Michael is the pastor of our church. What a fantastic coincidence! Darrel is voted in as the president of the youth group at my home church, and I am voted in as the vice president. Working in partnership with him, I develop basic leadership skills.

While I'm in school in Virginia, my parents and many of the youth have become involved in the Charismatic Movement. Some of my friends try to convince me that I am missing the power of the Holy Spirit evidenced by speaking in tongues. My desire is to have all God wants to give me, but I don't know what to think. I tell God my fears as well as my desires to be baptized in the Spirit and sense the presence of God in my life in greater ways.

I spend a lot of time with a mentoring couple in their home who treat me as though I'm a member of their family and invite me to drop in at any time of the day or night. Their belief and attentiveness to me personify God with skin on. They lead a youth Bible study in their home, and I make it a priority to attend. I experience such love and acceptance within this group. This couple encourages me to voice my thoughts and feelings and to pray honestly.

*****

Hopelessness in the Family

Two years after returning home from high school in Virginia, my family moves to a house out in the country that Dad has built. Since the lot, until the time of purchase, has been designated as forest land, Dad has removed as few trees as possible in building the house. I love the woods, especially at night. Walking out into the darkness, I leave behind the noise of yelling and chaos within the house. A sense of peace prevails as I drink in the fresh air and the stillness of the evening. The sliver of moonlight shimmering and dancing through the darkness of the forest has a mesmerizing effect on me. As I walk, the gentle movement of the trees cradles me, whispering, "You are safe here!" I often sing and dance along with the branches of the trees in the gentle breeze. In this sacred place, I find freedom to be me! In the stillness of this sanctuary, I belong and sense the Spirit of God.

Although Dad has built the walls of our house to keep out the darkness and dangers of the night, I long to escape the "normal" within the walls of our house to enjoy the darkness outside. I fear the rage inside my house and let go of any fear of the dark outside. I relax and breathe deeper in the forest, stand a bit taller, and feel a bit braver to reenter the house again.

The old familiar family patterns are still present for Miriam and me. One evening I arrive home to find Miriam lying across her bed in our shared bedroom, sobbing.

"How can God be a God of love and allow Mother to treat us and Dad this way? Mother acts so spiritual and quotes lots of scripture and gives all these prophetic words to people, but inside these walls, she goes into a rage for little things she doesn't like!"

"I struggle with her words and hurtful behavior as well. But what can we do about it?" I ask as we lay on the bed crying together.

Dad hears us talking when he gets up at 2:30 a.m. We express to him our perspectives regarding living at home again. Dad listens and says he understands and agrees with us. He offers no advice, though, nor does he model anything more than attempts to pacify Mother. *I wish Dad would stand up for us sometimes! He seems to feel as hopeless as we do. Why do I feel responsible to help our family?*

I express the idea of a family council to help us find some solution to our conflicts. Dad agrees to having the meeting. As we begin, I try to explain what I believe is happening within our family in terms of general conflict patterns. Within minutes, Mother is in tears. She begins yelling accusations. Dad says nothing. Mother is ill for the next three days, saying she has heart palpitations that keep her up at night.

"Sherill, if I die from a heart attack, it will be your fault! You've caused all of my heart problems!" Mother says in a high-pitched voice with a furrowed brow. She squeezes her eyes shut and grabs the left side of her chest as though she is holding her heart.

Fear seizes me as I try to imagine how I will live with myself if Mother dies. Am I really the one to blame for her heart problems? It is apparently hopeless and unattainable to have an open and free relationship with Mother.

*****

Although we have our struggles with Mother, we defend her if others criticize her. The elders of the charismatic church my parents are now attending come to our home one evening to confront Mother about some of her behaviors. They ask that I leave, but Mother states I am to stay. *Their accusations could send Mother into more heart troubles.* I stick up for her. Dad remains quiet. The elders don't have a broader perspective of Mother's need for mental and emotional treatment. They only confront her behavior, and that infuriates her further.

One evening, Mother attacks Dad physically. She slaps him harshly across the face and uses her fingernails to claw his face until he is bleeding. I am aghast watching and can't understand why Dad won't stick up for himself. Years later, I ask him about this incident. He says Mother has threatened off and on to call the police. Dad has feared Mother would somehow accuse him of abuse and the police would believe her.

7

Preparation for Africa

October 1974 to July 1979

OUR FOURTEEN-YEAR-OLD CAR IS purchased for $175 with cash we receive as wedding gifts. We are married in Florida at age twenty-two and spend our honeymoon in the North Carolina mountains at a friend's house trailer. We find many mice living under the bed we sleep in. Darrel says it is a blessing in disguise since they keep me in bed longer with him. Not romantic!

I glance at my handsome husband driving our red Volkswagen bug. His thick blond hair and physique have enticed many women to dream of dating him. Waves of gratitude surge through me for my marriage to such a passionate, adventurous, and spiritual man.

When we arrive at our first home in Virginia, Darrel jumps out of the car and runs around to the passenger side, opening my car door.

"I want to carry my bride over the threshold of our new home!"

"I'm no skinny bride, you know!"

My eyes scan the mint green, twenty-year-old house trailer in the field in front of me. We are renting it for $40 per month. The only other dwelling I see is a farmhouse up the road.

As I explore our eight-foot wide, forty-foot-long furnished home, my expectations are dampened. But *hey*, I tell myself, *I can live with anything. Even though I am an urban girl, I can learn to live in a field. The mint green curtains aren't my taste but putting up with them means I don't need to sew new curtains. The incredibly small kitchen only has three cupboards and a*

couple of drawers, but I can make do. I walk through the small bathroom to the bedroom. The bed only has three legs and is covered with dead flies. *Disgusting.*

"Darrel, how are we going to sleep in a bed with only three legs?"

"I'll fix it! Guess we'll have to prop it up temporarily with a pile of our books."

Darrel turns the refrigerator on, and I begin to fill it with the few groceries we have brought with us. When I pull the tray out under the small frozen section, I find a piece of meat with white maggots crawling over it. The stench is overwhelming. I gag with disgust as my stomach churns. The previous renters must have forgotten it when turning the refrigerator off. I call Darrel to dispose of it. With that image in my mind, it is time to cook dinner. All I can think of is macaroni and cheese now being a dish of cooked maggots.

During the next couple of days, we clean everything and move our wedding gifts inside. Then we are off to Pennsylvania for a few weeks to earn money for Darrel's college tuition by wallpapering and painting his brother's house. Someone should warn newlyweds that wallpapering puts your marriage to the test! When the strips of wallpaper don't match perfectly or bubbles appear, it is always the other person's fault.

Upon returning to our trailer, we discover the pipes have frozen and burst while we've been gone. The whole reservoir of water for the farm and our water supply has drained into our trailer. Now we have no water. My heart sinks because some of our wedding gifts are completely ruined. What a mess!

This is just the beginning of our adventures in the trailer. While I'm in bed, I hear scraping sounds like fingernails on a blackboard. A family of possums live under the trailer. They sharpen their teeth at night on the pipes under our bed.

While Darrel attends Eastern Mennonite College, I work in the admissions office and communications center. Darrel often returns to the library after supper to study. When it is quiet in the trailer, a family of mice come out to play in the living room. I put my feet up on a chair and watch them. We try to kill them with traps, but we soon give up. The mice outnumber those we trap several times over because we live in a field. One evening Darrel stands on a chair with a brick, and I use a yardstick to stir up the mice clan. Dropping a brick to kill a mouse is like throwing a shoe across the room to kill a fly on the opposite wall. Futile to say the least.

The first winter in the trailer is exceptionally cold. The water freezes underground, so without water, we can't use the toilet. I learn to do my business outside off the porch in the snow. It is like sailors using the stern of a ship as a "poop deck." We buy a plastic garbage can to fill with water, so I have water to cook and flush the toilet. And we heat water for baths and washing dishes. Then the toilet quits working. The landlord is on a trip. Darrel and Uncle Michael take the toilet outside and try to fix it. The result? Sewage water backs up into the kitchen sink. This is the last straw for me. I have had it!

"Darrel, I am done adapting to this primitive living! I can't cope with this anymore! You keep promising me it will get better and then it gets worse. Living in a camper might be more pleasant than this." I vent. "You love risk and adventure, but the escapades in this adventure of living in this trailer are too much for me."

So, we move into the upstairs apartment of Aunt Peggy and Uncle Michael's house until the ground thaws.

*****

On our next visit to Florida, Darrel goes dumpster diving behind carpet stores. We transport large amounts of carpet scraps back to Virginia in our VW bug. I cut them into strips, creating twelve-inch patterned squares of complimentary colors. I stack the numerous squares I create in boxes. In my mind I envision a living room carpet created from the squares.

One bitterly cold windy evening, I use a strong glue from an open two-gallon container to attach the carpet squares onto thick brown paper that is cut to fit the floor in the trailer. The kerosene furnace is lit, and I'm hoping the trailer warms up while I work.

After a couple of hours, I have a throbbing headache, but I push myself to finish the area I am working on. When I finally stand up to leave, I struggle to think clearly. My dizziness scares me. I make my way up to the nearby farmhouse and explain to the man who answers the door that I need help. He calls Darrel saying, "Your wife is incoherent."

Aunt Peggy calls the poison center at the hospital, and the doctor instructs her to tell everyone in the house except me to put on a winter coat, open the windows, and then wait until I come off my "high" from glue sniffing. Coming down from the high feels like hammers pounding my head, so sleep eludes me. What a way to learn about accidentally becoming high. I can't imagine why young people choose to sniff glue.

*****

When the weather turns warmer, we return to our trailer and the drama continues. During a thunderstorm, I sit petrified on our small couch and watch a ball of fire come out of the kitchen light fixture. Not the type of fireworks I want to see. We never do learn why, though we suspect there are some problems with the electric wiring.

The oven door won't stay completely shut. Darrel instructs me to use duct tape to close it and to wedge a chair between the oven and the furnace when I want to bake. If I need to go to the bathroom or bedroom while baking, I climb over the barricade.

While we are on a trip, a rat eats through the wood in the bathroom wall and chews a large portion of the seal off the refrigerator door. He also eats holes in the "lovely" mint green curtains in the living room. I am not used to living like this as my carpenter father prided himself in having a house that is well built.

In our five years of dating, Darrel and I had written many letters to each other. In the last three years before preparing for our wedding, we had only been together in person for a total of six weeks. Darrel had hitchhiked across Europe and the Sahara Desert to visit his parents who were serving as mission workers in Nigeria. Then he and his brother had hitchhiked through many countries in Africa prior to Darrel attending a mission training school in Glasgow, Scotland for two years. We had processed a lot about our dreams and goals in life through letters.

I shared with Darrel in a letter in October 1972: "For a long time I've sensed you will be going back to Africa to serve in missions. I've imagined you and me together in Africa as well. Darrel, I don't know much about living in rural Africa, and you are probably right that I wouldn't be able to handle it if I was plopped down there right now. This I do know, though, that whether God leads us together or leads us each to someone else, I will never be satisfied to just get married here in the States, raise a family, and have a job. I sense God is calling me to a different kind of life. If God leads us together, I am willing to follow God's leading to Africa. I know I have no idea what all it will involve or the sacrifices that will need to be made, but I know that if that is God's will for us, I will be happy."

It is one thing to make strong statements in letters. It is another to live them! More than two years later, we find that our marital arguments are often over things that happen in the trailer.

"Honey, God is using these trials to prepare you for living in Africa," he says.

"I'm not in Africa! I'm living in the United States. And we don't need to live like we're already in Africa. I can face Africa when I get there. And I do not need a preacher husband!" I respond in a louder voice than I intend.

"I thought you learned to live with a lack of resources when you were in Youth With A Mission (YWAM)," Darrel says. "You told me you learned to adapt to anything that happened along the way."

"That is because while I was in YWAM, there weren't other options. We don't have to live like this."

*****

Darrel had learned about YWAM from a Christian magazine advertisement. He had encouraged me to attend their nine-month program before our wedding. It seemed beneficial for me as their discipleship program was a great training for mission workers. So, I quit my job, sold my car, and bought an airplane ticket to Switzerland.

People attending the training were from at least fifteen countries and as many denominations. During a class session, one of the teachers prayed for each student. When it was my turn, she was silent for a few minutes.

"I sense you have built walls around your heart as protection. But it has also resulted in you often feeling alone in a remote inner realm. I don't know why these walls were needed as a defense mechanism for safety in your life, but they are now becoming obstacles for you." Then she prayed for those walls to come down. I longed to be as free, authentic, and open to others in the way that she prayed. I learned in YWAM to accept God's love and grace and see myself the way my Creator does rather than trying to prove that I am good enough for God. What freedom!

Part of the training included a three-month Middle East trip, traveling in an old school bus with fifty students and staff. We slept in large tents that held thirty people and did our own cooking over campfire stoves. I was the leader for the lunch crew. We learned how to adapt even when our campground was flooded or muddy because of heavy rain or we could not find bathroom facilities while traveling and had to use the sides of the road. When our vehicles broke down or we were held up at border crossings for hours at a time with no explanation, learning flexibility was key.

The last two months of the training involved a summer of service. For my outreach, I flew to Ethiopia with one other student to partner with the Mennonite church there. I assisted in delivering babies, binding books, and sewing medical supplies.

*****

In living in the trailer, however, arguments with Darrel leave me emotionally triggered about what I should be able to accept or cope with due to my training. Somehow God and Darrel know ahead of time that I'm just not good enough or ready for missions. I sometimes overreact when I'm triggered. Then Darrel shuts down and becomes silent, and I'm left feeling the weight of our unhealthy communication. Oh, the joy of finding our way as a couple.

Despite our different perspectives, we do make wonderful memories living in the trailer. Darrel, as the world's most romantic man, invites me to stargaze outside on a blanket or cooks me a special candlelit meal with soothing music playing in the background. Whenever we are at home together after supper, we lay on the couch and talk about our day.

*****

To save money, we don't leave the furnace on during the day when we are at work or college. It takes a while for the trailer to warm up after we return, so I often fix supper while wearing my winter coat.

In our first year of marriage, Mother and Dad visit us in the trailer. Prior to their arrival, before taking a shower, Darrel lights the furnace to warm up the trailer. After showering, he checks the furnace while he is still naked and finds it hasn't lit successfully. He opens the door and throws in a lit match. The kerosene fumes instantly explode and blow black ash all over Darrel and throughout the trailer.

"Darrel, are you okay?" I yell while running to him.

"I'm not sure! I think it singed the hair off my body! And you've always said you loved me being a hairy man!" Darrel says.

What a sight! My naked husband is covered with ash from head to foot. I can't stop laughing at the sight of him. If we touch the ash, it smudges into our skin, or into the carpet. Therefore, the only way to clean up the mess is to vacuum Darrel's body, the curtains, hanging pictures, furniture, etc. A memory we will never forget!

Somehow, we keep creating messes at inappropriate times. We clean the trailer the best we can before my parents arrive. We give Mother and Dad our bed, and we sleep on the studio couch in the living room. Soon after cuddling together on one side, the couch dumps us onto the floor like the wild horse that bucked me off his back when I was a teenager. Mother and Dad must have heard the loud noise, but they never say a word about it in the morning.

*****

While Darrel studies, I often struggle with loneliness in the evenings. We investigate the financial scenario for both of us to attend college because we realize it's going to be years before we both graduate. We learn that it's cheaper for us to attend college together than to do it separately. I can still use the scholarship offered to me years earlier and Darrel receives grants. So, I jump into the nursing program. Sometimes, though, we don't have cash for groceries. One day I lament to God about our lack of income. When opening the mailbox, I find a card with a check from friends. I am learning more about trusting God's provision in hard times.

In April 1978, I graduate from college with a nursing degree. We celebrate my accomplishment of being the only one in my family to graduate from a four-year college. I take my state nursing board exams in July in a building without air conditioning while being eight months pregnant. My in-utero-son kicks the table rhythmically while I lean over the papers in front of me to mark my answers. If only he could kick in a coded manner to help me choose the correct answers. I receive confirmation weeks later that I've passed the state board tests. I'm so relieved and grateful.

I give birth to Obe in August; it is the hardest thing I have ever done as well as the most exhilarating. What joy Darrel and I have in examining his perfectly formed body. We are so grateful that friends offer to pay the hospital bill as our student health insurance does not cover pregnancy. A couple in our congregation rents us their two-bedroom apartment off the back of their house. What a gift!

Since Darrel is attending Seminary and teaching part-time, he and I can be flexible in caring for Obe. In the summer of 1979, I work the second shift part-time at the hospital, on the pediatric floor, to gain work experience before we leave for Nigeria.

As we prepare to serve in Nigeria, we believe God will provide for us and intervene on our behalf in ways beyond what we can imagine. Like the children's song, God is so big, strong, and mighty, and there's nothing God cannot do. Of course, there is nothing God cannot do *for us*.

We just need to trust!

8

Processing My Broken God Image and Self-Image

1980 to 1983

WHEN WE RETURN FROM Nigeria at age twenty-eight, we live temporarily with our friends, Elam and Harriet, in Harrisonburg, Virginia. After four weeks, we move to a small two-bedroom apartment on the first floor of a renovated chicken house. I take a part-time job as a home health nurse to support us financially.

Rene's first seizure as an infant became the first of many seizures that sometimes happen daily now. Rene, at six-months-old, goes unconscious three to four times a day. When we describe Rene's episodes to the doctor, he wonders if she is holding her breath when she is stressed. He says Rene appears to have a low threshold for seizure activity, and therefore, the breath holding puts her over the threshold and triggers a seizure. The pediatrician concludes from further tests that her high bilirubin after birth must have damaged the temporal lobe of her brain, resulting in epilepsy.

Darrel returns to Eastern Mennonite Seminary to finish his degree. He reflects on our Nigerian experience as part of his study. We discuss together how we might have requested doing things differently in the beginning in learning more of the language and culture prior to Darrel teaching at the school. We conclude it would have been better if we had depended more on the school's principal to teach us cultural ways rather than hearing things first from our mission friends.

No matter how much we thought we had prepared ourselves for living in Nigeria, we were not prepared for the depth of pain we experienced in those fifteen months. We sense a need to process our God image. I seek out books to read that deal with a theology of suffering.

One evening as Darrel and I are sipping tea together on the couch, I admit my inner wrestling. "Darrel, I'm really struggling with our decision to give birth to Rene without adequate resources, which the doctor says caused her epilepsy. It would be easier for me to accept if I felt like our being in Nigeria made a difference."

"I'm sorry. I'm struggling with a lot of what happened as well."

"If God wanted to test us, God could have continued that here in the United States in living in the trailer!" I say. "At least we would have had good healthcare. I feel guilty for not demanding that we leave near the time of delivery to ensure adequate healthcare for Rene's birth."

"Hindsight is always 20/20 vision," Darrel says. "We were making decisions with a lot of unknowns. Yes, if we would have known what we now understand, we would have made different choices."

One Sunday in church, the leader uses the phrase, "God is in control, so we don't need to worry about anything." I do not even attempt to listen to the rest of the service. *I have heard this phrase repeated many times in my life. What does it really mean? Yes, God is sovereign overall, but God has given humans dominion over the earth. And no one can deny that there is much suffering in the world. Have we created an image of God that we desire as humans, a God that supposedly pulls all the puppet strings and makes things happen for us? Maybe free will is more important to God than being in total control.*

On the drive home, I process with Darrel. "If God was in control of everything that happened in Nigeria, then I don't know if I want to trust God with my life, and I definitely don't want to go back overseas."

"There is no way that God was controlling everything that happened in Nigeria. People do make choices, including us," Darrel says.

"Well, then I must wrestle with what I was always taught about God. I had some idea of what I may face in missions, but what happened in Nigeria was beyond my imagination. If this is what a call to missions means, then I will have to reconsider saying yes to this direction for our lives."

Darrel's raised eyebrows reveal his concern as he listens.

"I'm grateful for God's answer to our prayer in having Tamara pray for Obe when he was seriously ill. That assured me that God knew our situation," I continue. "But I'm wrestling with the bigger picture of all that happened in Nigeria. If I could believe that God grieves with us over what happened in Nigeria rather than being in total control, then I could possibly risk trusting God again in an overseas assignment."

It's scary to let go of some of my certainties about God. How do I know what to hold on to and what to let go of? After attending one year at an Assembly of God Bible college after high school, I mull questions about faith and healing. Does God always heal when we pray in faith? When people aren't healed, is it really because they didn't have enough faith? I'm more aware of evil forces in the world and an acute need to pray against the power of darkness in the name of Jesus. What will the result be if I'm not faithful to pray in this way? How responsible am I in this partnership with God in building the kingdom?

Months after our return to the United States, I have a dream that we travel back to Nigeria on a visitor's visa and then are not allowed to leave due to the political situation. I am surprised by how friendly, kind, and thoughtful the principal and his wife are to us. If we meet them in the future, I want to believe that it could be different.

*****

Two days after we return from a visit to my parents in Florida, Dad calls. "Sherill, you need to apologize to your mother for your disrespectful comments regarding her wanting me to talk to our neighbor about their poisonous bushes."

I sigh and distract myself by preparing dinner while I talk, as I know from experience this could be a frustrating conversation.

"Dad, we've had these conversations often after we visit you and Mother," I say while chopping onions. "Mother's fears are unrealistic, and you know it." She wants me to agree with her that the neighbor's bushes are causing her distressing physical symptoms. And she is convinced that the neighbor's tree will fall on their bedroom roof, so she wants Dad to demand the tree be cut down. I have tried to help her examine her fears.

"You're not really going to talk to the neighbors, are you?" I ask.

I strain to hear his answer. "I already did," Dad says in a low voice.

"How embarrassing. I bet the neighbors were quite agreeable to her demand, right?"

"No, but at least I got Mother off my back about that demand. So, will you please apologize to Mother?" Dad asks again in a whinny voice.

"Dad, there is nothing for me to apologize for in this situation."

Silence.

"Then can you do it for my sake so I can have some peace?"

"I don't know." I have given in to this argument "for Dad's sake" so many times already. This time I can't bring myself to make that phone call.

*****

Darrel notices that I'm a different person when I'm with Mother. He describes it as "my strings are taut as though they might snap." When Mother negatively critiques me or tries to get her way through guilt manipulation, he recognizes that I'm internally triggered. My relationship with Mother affects our marriage and Darrel wants stronger boundaries in our relationship with her. He is hesitant to bring up frustrations in our marriage as it often triggers my feelings of not being good enough for him.

As a result, I start meeting with a professional counselor to work on my family of origin issues. When we tell Uncle Michael and Aunt Peggy that I am seeing a counselor, they tell me stories about Mother I have never heard. *Uncle Michael had been our family's first pastor when we moved from Ohio to Florida.*

"Sherill, your mother was paranoid and had mental and emotional struggles already when you moved to Florida when you were in the third grade," he explains. "She accused me of ignoring her when she was in line to greet me after a service. She was super sensitive and lived in an unreal world of her own because of her paranoia. She also stirred up others in the church by creating conflict."

Ouch! My mother created conflict beyond our family!

"I'm so sorry!" I have known Uncle Michael and Aunt Peggy for many years, and they don't speak negatively about people. I know instinctively that they are telling me this for my benefit.

*****

During a visit to Florida, the pastor of the third church my parents are attending asks to speak with Darrel and me privately in his office. He strongly encourages us to assist my mother in obtaining medical help for her mental illness.

"Sherill, your mother needs help. I will never again allow your mother to speak to me in my office without a tape recorder running or another person present as a witness."

"What do you think my mother's diagnosis may be if I can get her to a doctor?"

"I'm not a psychiatrist. But, from what I've experienced of your mother, I think she may have paranoid schizophrenia."

All of this is difficult for me to process; it hasn't occurred to me that Mother could appear functional, lucid, and persuasive, yet have a mental illness. It partially validates why I struggle to have a healthy relationship with Mother.

I schedule an appointment for Mother to be seen by a doctor. She normally doesn't see medical doctors. And though I have requested that the doctor's office not call to confirm her appointment, they do anyway. Mother answers the call, cancels the appointment, and is furious.

"There is nothing wrong with me! It's your father who needs help!" she says.

"Mother, we would appreciate if you would talk to a doctor. You and Dad can go together." I explain.

"I hope and pray that you have a disrespectful daughter like you someday. Then you will understand what it feels like to be your mother." She walks away muttering under her breath.

We never succeed in getting Mother to a doctor. No matter what diagnosis Mother may have been given, her paranoia would most likely have prevented it ever being treated.

As part of my inner healing work, I decide to interview my parents if Darrel accompanies me. I create interview questions with the help of my counselor. When my parents visit us, we take them to a restaurant with a private cozy room and the warmth of a fire near our table. I explain that I desire to learn more about their lives. Mother's wrinkled brow, set jaw, and folded arms indicate her lack of trust, though she does answer the questions with short responses.

I learn quite a bit that evening. Mother speaks about being bullied by her brothers and being forced to do hard farm labor while her father drove into town to buy more liquor. With a tremor in her voice, she says her father had forced her to quit school after eighth grade to work in the fields. Dad speaks about his father being harsh and sometimes cruel to his mother. He says that he had vowed as a young boy to never treat his wife in the way his father had modeled. I validate the pain they have experienced from their families of origin. I tell Mother how sorry I am that she has an unfulfilled dream of attending high school.

As I process this information further in counseling, I wonder if when I don't agree with Mother, it triggers memories of her brothers bullying her. I come to understand that Mother interprets events abnormally. This results in disordered thinking and behavior that impairs her ability to build

effective relationships. I put myself in Mother's shoes and find myself grieving many losses she has experienced in life.

Accepting that Mother is not emotionally and mentally well is more of
a journey than a moment in time. I grieve the "never will be's." Most of all, I
grieve that I will never have the intimate and close relationship with Mother
that I have dreamed about my whole life.

Part of acceptance means I need to release Mother from what she
can't give me and to stop seeking her love and affirmation. In letting go,
I begin learning to love and accept myself for who I am, an imperfect, yet
lovable person. I learn that adults have automatic brain grooves from patterned thinking. The good news is that we can create new brain grooves
with practice. So, I focus on the positive true thoughts about myself. This
isn't a quick or one-time fix, but rather a longer journey of recognizing my
negative thinking in the moment. Eventually my positive thought habits
replace the negative ones.

*The counselor helped me understand that I had accepted Christ out of
fear rather than love. The fear of hell added to my image of God as the big man
with the stick up in Heaven who was always watching how I was behaving. I
had projected my experience with my mother onto my image of God.*

With time, I understand I have allowed my identity, self-esteem, and
emotional landscape to be defined by Mother's emotions, words, and actions. Now I can embrace my capacity to author my own story about myself,
God, and life.

Interactions with Darrel's extended family also bring healing to me.
My parents-in-law and Darrel's siblings and spouses accept and love me for
who I am.

*****

A Japanese art form, *Wabi Sabi*, mends broken pottery using resin laced
with gold or silver. The flaw is seen as a unique part of the object's history,
which adds to its beauty. What a powerful image of transforming brokenness and suffering into beauty!

*I had tried for years to reach my ideal of perfection, to be enough. But
the goal kept moving. I learned to befriend my inner brokenness and to honor
the scars. In doing so, I laced those imperfections, brokenness, and scars with
gold and silver, creating my own inner beauty from the pain and brokenness
of the past.*

*****

While visiting Darrel's parents in December 1982, we hear about an opportunity with a different mission agency to partner with African Indigenous Church leaders in Swaziland, Southern Africa. We are intrigued and ask more questions.

We learn that the Zionist leaders are requesting assistance in leadership development among their churches. The Zionists are one of 6,500 indigenous Christian movements within Africa. The name "Zionists" comes from Zion as used in scripture. It is not connected with the country of Israel.

We cautiously explore this opportunity as there are caveats for us in considering another assignment overseas. One of our priorities is the availability of excellent medical resources for our children, as we are not willing to risk our children's health again. Another priority is time given for language and culture learning prior to the day-to-day job expected of us. South Africa has top-rated healthcare, and we will be able to see specialists if we need them. The agency informs us that language learning is one of their top priorities as well.

It seems like a good fit for us. There are in-country supervisors who will walk with us in getting settled. We prepare to leave the United States and move to Swaziland. As part of our preparation, we attend a beneficial language acquisition program in Michigan.

We leave Virginia in August 1983 with our four-year-old son and three-year-old daughter.

Time to risk again. . .

PART II

New Perspectives of God
Swaziland, Southern Africa
(Swaziland Was Renamed
Eswatini in April 2018)
1983 to 1991

To know God demands that we
be willing to be touched by
Divine Love.
To be touched by God's love
is to be forever changed.
To surrender to Divine Love
is to find our soul's home –
The place and identity for which
we yearn in every cell of our being.

—*The Gift of Being Yourself: The Sacred Call to*
Self-Discovery by David G. Benner

9

Creator of Diversity

ROLLING HILLS AND PLATEAUS, palm trees and thorn trees, lush forests and grasslands dot the landscape of the diverse country of Swaziland. Some call Swaziland the "Switzerland of Africa." Though a small country, the Swazis have been a homogeneous entity for over three hundred years. Perhaps this has given them the self-confidence to accept others without fear of losing their own identity. The Swazi people have never been at war with Whites and have a history of peace-seeking. After being a British protectorate for some years with a policy of minimal involvement, it has been a sovereign state since 1968. Swaziland, now called Eswatini since 2018, is a kingdom with a reigning king, an absolute monarch.

*****

Two Zionist leaders welcome us at the airport with hospitable embraces. As part of our orientation to Swaziland, we travel to a Zionist church built near a church leader's home on a hillside. The pastor, dressed in a green robe with a white stole over his shoulder and wrapped around his waist, greets us at the door. The small, cement-block church holds more people than we initially think possible. Male leaders and their wives sit in chairs across the front, facing the congregants, with men on the right and women on the left. The congregants sit on low benches or on the straw-covered floor, matching the separation of the genders modeled by the leaders.

The congregants arrive wearing white robes with blue or green sashes. Outside the door, everyone removes their shoes, and we add ours to the growing pile off to the side. Just as Moses takes off his sandals because God says he was standing on holy ground (Exodus 3:5), Zionists view the space inside the church as holy ground. Many of the adults enter with head-height wooden staffs topped with a cross. They take Jesus's words literally to take up their crosses and follow him (Luke 9:23).

The leader belts out a line of a song, and the people sing an echo in response, using the pentatonic scale, a five-note rather than a seven-note scale. The antiphonal singing continues until the leader brings it to a close. They sing with enthusiasm and celebration.

People bring their offering money to the front and drop their coins in a large metal bowl. The loud ping of the coins adds percussion sounds in

rhythm with the singing. Men and women rise and join others to sing and dance their way to the front, meandering around people sitting on the floor. They give coins, not just once, but many times until they have no more. Some put in a bill and take out coins in change so they can continue to sing and dance. We join in celebration with awkward movements since dancing is not a part of our church repertoire.

The leader preaches from the scripture and then sits down. Both men and women stand to add on to the sermon. If a person speaks too long, someone in the audience interrupts by starting a song. We learn that this is the culturally acceptable way to nudge the speaker to conclude the speech.

A minister invites people to come to the front for prayer for physical healing. One woman comes forward. Leaders gather around her with their staffs. A man pokes the part of the body needing healing with the end of his staff. *It looks to me like he is adding to her pain.* Another leader vigorously shakes the woman by the shoulders. *Don't think I'll be asking for prayer!* We learn later that the leaders view their "roughness" as necessary confrontation of the devil for the woman to be freed.

Whenever a person prays during the service, someone closes the door and pulls wooden shutters over the open windows. Jesus says in scripture, when people pray, they should go into their room and close the door (Matthew 6:6).

After the four-hour service, the congregants search for their shoes, greet one another, and wind their way back down the hillside. I feel relief that Obe and Rene have endured the four-hour service without being too distracting. These services are new for all of us, and we find them intriguing, although a little anxiety producing as well. I wonder if I will be expected to do things that I will find awkward or uncomfortable.

After congregants disperse, the pastor and his wife invite us into their home for bread and tea. This family displays warmth and interest in assisting us to learn more about the culture and their church. We recognize that the Zionist services maintain more traditional Swazi culture and practice than what we had observed in the Nigerian Independent churches. Rather than school buildings, like in Nigeria, Zionists in Swaziland have a school without walls called Faith Bible School. They often hold all-night services and seminars in church buildings or schools because their income is limited.

Whatever we bring as input needs to be culturally adapted to their understanding and practices. We pray for openness to the positive influence the Zionists will have on us. Our hearts are full of gratitude for the incredible mentors we have in Swaziland, both Swazi colleagues and wise agency supervisors. They help us process our role and relationship-building with the Zionists.

*****

Language Learning

We enroll in an intensive Siswati language-learning program for four weeks, while living at a denominational church retreat center. The Zionist leaders find a tutor to further help us in learning the SiSwati language. Our tutor, Lomali, a seventeen-year-old pregnant girl, attends night school to complete her high school education. She comes to our house five days a week for three hours a day. We take responsibility for what we want to learn each day, focusing on the language we need to speak in daily life. While we have our language lessons, Obe and Rene attend a nearby preschool. They learn SiSwati songs and greetings at the school. Obe comes home and says, "I'll teach you the language!" *If only we could learn the language as quickly as our children do.*

Every day we try to find people to converse with in SiSwati. Those who agree to listen to our little SiSwati speeches and engage in conversation with us are gracious and encouraging in our slow progress. The Siswati language includes different clicks of the tongue for the letters "c," "q," and "x." Words include the subject, verb, and object. This results in words being up to twenty-six letters long. I find it easier to hear and understand SiSwati than to voice what I want to say. I must form the long words ahead of time in my head before I begin to speak at all.

Language learning humbles us. Darrel encourages Lomali to explain some things in English for my understanding since she wants to improve her English in mutual language learning. One day, he thinks he is saying in SiSwati to her, "Try, try, try." Unconsciously, he adds a click of the tongue and, in fact, commands her to urinate three times.

Lomali stands up and says in English, "I think I will," while walking to the bathroom. We all laugh. *I wonder how many times we say inappropriate things in SiSwati and people are too nice to laugh or respond like Lomali does.*

The language is tonal, and a mistake can be disastrous and embarrassing. Darrel later speaks at a church where he describes being with his "girlfriend" rather than his wife. People laugh and Darrel is confused, so he stops and asks someone to explain. Then he corrects himself and laughs with them.

Darrel learns from a Swazi colleague how to speak his love for me in SiSwati. Because the children or other expatriate (foreign) adults do not understand what he is saying, he repeats these "sweet nothings" to me aloud in their presence. Sometimes he adds that it's time to close off the evening because he wants to make love to me. I warn him that someday he is going to make wrong assumptions, and then we will both be embarrassed!

My confidence in speaking SiSwati often tumbles in my feeble attempts to be understood. I wish I could be like the lilac-breasted roller, a common bird in Swaziland. When it jumps off a tree branch, it loops and tumbles toward the ground with wings almost closed. All the while, its bright colors of green, pink, lilac, and blue flash in the sunlight. Before hitting the ground, the bird flaps its wings open and quickly flies straight up to the open sky. I desire to find my wings in speaking and understanding the language. But for now, my tumbling, loopy way of speaking will have to do.

*****

Family Experiences

Our first home is a small, two-bedroom house within walking distance of downtown Manzini, the second largest city in Swaziland. The house needs a lot of repairs, including plumbing, painting, and clearing metal and broken machines out of the yard.

The mosquitoes are delighted that we have moved in. The first night, Obe and Rene are still awake at 11:00 p.m. due to mosquitoes biting them. It is hot and sticky, and our windows have no screens. Mosquitoes pepper Rene's whole body with bites, twelve on just one cheek. We have not experienced mosquitoes earlier, as we have been staying at higher elevations with cooler weather. The way to keep mosquitoes away when you have no screens is to burn coils in each bedroom at night. The green mosquito coils, lit with a match, slowly burn for seven hours. Mosquitoes do not like the smoke from the coil, so they look for others to bother.

The next day, someone starts a brush fire among tall weeds across the road from our new home. The wind picks up and soon smoke is coming out of the building on the property. We don't have a telephone, so Darrel runs to a neighbor to call for help. Firemen spray water as quickly as possible, but it is not enough. The building burns to the ground. That evening, we have no electricity because of the fire. We look around our kitchen and realize we don't have any candles or oil lamps. Our orientation has not included the list of necessities to always have available. We are now learning the hard way. In the coming weeks, we introduce ourselves to our Swazi neighbors. They are welcoming and open to all our questions.

Five months later, we attend a retreat in Lesotho, a landlocked country surrounded by South Africa. On our return, the landlord informs us that we need to be out of the house in one week because the house is being sold. We hear later that the landlord decides to rent the house to a new employee. Though we have a two-year signed lease, the landlord does not honor it. Once again, we are homeless! To make matters worse, our in-country supervisor is in Canada. *This feels like a pattern in our lives! It takes so much energy to move and make a house homey for the family. We just need some stability!*

Our in-country supervisor has promised us a larger house when a couple completes their time of service in six months. So, we visit this couple and risk asking them if we could possibly move into their house now for the sake of our children's adjustment. Their initial response is negative, but later they come back saying they are willing to move into a smaller house next door. We open the fence between the properties so that we can go back and forth to each other's houses easily. Three days after Christmas, we pack and move. This couple's willingness to allow us to move once instead of twice in the next six months is the best Christmas present ever! And over the remaining months they live next door to us, we become great friends.

The new house, situated on a hill, has a beautiful view of the mountains in the distance. Obe and Rene delight in playing on the large rocks on the property. Banana, papaya, guava, avocado, mulberry, orange, and macadamia trees fill the yard. We love all the fruit trees around the house, but so do the snakes. Several times, we find spitting cobras ready to strike outside our front door in the foliage.

The children find many friends in our neighborhood, both from other countries as well as Swazis. We often have ten children playing together in the yard, in the sandbox, on the rocks, or using the tire swing. A couple years later, we add a tree house and a trampoline. We develop relationships with other families and plan outings to animal game parks where we see rhino, giraffe, zebra, antelope, and ostriches. Hiking with other families enables us to make new friends while getting exercise at the same time. Life is good and full of joy and meaning.

Obe and Rene playing with friends in the sandbox in our yard

Cultural Dilemmas

The children wake on a Sunday morning to the sound of Darrel practicing his SiSwati sermon.

"I don't want to go to a Zionist church today," Obe complains. "The service is way too long! Why aren't we going to the church with my Sunday School?"

"I usually take you to your Sunday School. But today we're taking some visitors with us who want to experience a Zionist service," I say. "Why don't you help me pack some books and toys for when the service gets too long for you?"

We hurriedly gather what may keep the children occupied outside the small block church building when their patience runs out in the service. I pack snacks and drinks for them since the service will last from mid-morning until mid-afternoon.

Prior to the service, I ask if I can sit in the back of the church rather than complying with their tradition that guests sit up-front as a gesture of honor. I hope that this time our guests can sit up-front, and I can sit in the back. Then Obe and Rene will not be a distraction to the whole congregation.

"No, *Make* (Mrs.) Hostetter. You are the *umfundisi's* (minister's) wife. You must sit up-front."

Obe, age six, and Rene, age four, understand our guidelines. They need to sit quietly at my feet for one hour to show respect before they can go outside. Rene doesn't really sit still anywhere. She bounces with energy all day. The church services hold Swazi children's attention. For our children, it is a marathon of endurance because they don't understand the language.

"Is the time up yet?" Obe asks me not just once, but three times, in the first forty-five minutes of the service.

"No," I whisper. "I'll let you know when you can go outside."

Obe and Rene stretch out their legs while sitting on the floor up-front, then they push each other to gain more of their own personal space. I finally tell them they may leave the service. One of our guests' daughters, Amy, who is older than our children, goes out with them.

No aisle exists in a Zionist church because everyone except the leaders is sitting on the floor or side benches. There are no empty spaces. Not long after Rene leaves the service, she returns, weaving her way among the women to reach me up-front.

Before she is even near me, she says in her normal, loud voice with a cookie in one hand, "I have to go potty, and I can't find the toilet paper."

I wait until she gets close to me and whisper, "The toilet paper is in the green bag. Please stay outside and play. Ask your friend, Amy, for help if you're having a problem, okay?" I have never succeeded in teaching Rene how to whisper, but I emphasize to her she needs to use her quiet voice.

A special choir gathers to sing for the guests. They form a half-circle across the front facing all of us on chairs, rather than the seated congregation. While they are singing, Rene comes back in and struggles to find a way to reach me through the women seated on the floor. She chooses instead to go to Darrel on the other side. In the process, she trips over a cassette player recording the choir. She lands at the feet of the older Zionist leaders up-front. *How embarrassing!*

Darrel grabs her arm to pull her to her feet. She says, "Daddy, Obe spilled his drink in the back of the truck!"

Darrel whispers instructions to Rene for cleaning up the mess.

Before the service is over, Rene makes one more dramatic appearance.

"Mommy, Obe broke a window in the truck and there is glass everywhere!"

This time, holding Rene's hand, we weave through the seated women and out the door. All eyes follow us.

Is it worth it for me to go to these churches with Darrel? I'm not sure. Do people even hear the message?

After the service, I approach a Zionist woman, "I'm sorry my children were such a distraction today. How do you get your children to sit still for so many hours?"

"They know they must sit still, or they will be beaten."

How does spanking a child to sit still in church affect their image of God? Obe already believes that church is an endurance test. But from the perspective of the local culture, our children are being disrespectful. Oh, how do we navigate these cultural dilemmas that arise from different values and norms?

*****

I remember my initial shock in being in South Africa, the large country that borders Swaziland. The public swimming pool has a sign that says, "For Whites Only." While at the beach in Durban, Obe asks, "Mom, why are there no Blacks swimming at this beach? The only Blacks here are serving drinks or selling food to the Whites."

"Oh, you are right, Obe!" I say after looking all around us. "Darrel, why don't you and Obe walk back to the road and look for any signs about who can use this beach?"

"Sure," Obe says. He always enjoys detective work to solve a mystery.

"Mom, this is a Whites-only beach!" Obe reports on his return.

"That doesn't match our values. We'll have to find an international beach on this stretch of road," Darrel says.

"But first I need to use the restroom," I reply.

To find a public restroom, I must walk back to the road. I find that even the restrooms are segregated, marked for Whites, Blacks, Coloreds, and Asians. Out of principle, I don't want to go into a Whites-only restroom where my Swazi friends can never go. So, I try going into the Asian one. But I am stopped right inside the door. An Asian woman sitting on a chair inside the entrance states that I am not allowed to use an Asian restroom. I can only go into the "Whites" restroom. Though I am uncomfortable with my white privilege, I must give in to the system of segregation. There is no choice.

We search until we find an international beach and continue to use it every time we vacation in Durban. We decide to only stay overnight in places that allow Blacks to use the premises, even if it costs more. I keep reminding myself that the United States has a history of segregated pools, beaches, hotels, and restaurants even into the middle of the twentieth century.

I'm grateful that Swaziland does not have this system of segregation by race, known as Apartheid. South Africa has developed Apartheid, basing it partly on their interpretation of scripture that says the children of Ham became "hewers of wood and drawers of water." (Joshua 9:21) Apartheid affects who can use specific restaurants, restrooms, schools, and other public amenities. Swaziland is a much smaller nation and Blacks have the highest percentage of the population, so we as Whites are a minority in the country. South Africa is governed by Whites while Swaziland is governed by Blacks.

10

Lavish Host

To IMMERSE OURSELVES FURTHER in the language and culture, we ask the Zionist leaders if we can live with a Swazi Zionist family for two weeks to converse in SiSwati all day. The Zionist family they choose for our immersion experience speaks only a couple words of English. They live in the brown-covered mountains of Mankayane. Alfred Msibi and his family farm four acres of land for their living and sell their vegetables locally. We worry about their expectations of us and our children, though we trust we will find our way.

Alfred and Emellinah Msibi

The Msibi family must have anxiety about our expectations of them as well. To the side of the latrine, they have built a mud enclosure around an old bathtub so we can use buckets of water in a private bathing space. The water then drains out a pipe to the outside. The Msibis have transformed old car seats into swings for Obe and Rene by painting them and hanging them from a tree branch near the front of their house.

In this area, the houses are often beehive-shaped huts made of mud, sticks, and stones with a grass thatched roof. Other people have cement-block houses. The Msibis have a combination of both on their homestead, and they generously give a cement-block bedroom to our family. The hospitality of the Msibis overwhelms and challenges us. *Would we go to such efforts to host them?*

We learn that the Msibi family have seven children, two of them still living at home. They have quite a few grandchildren as well and are raising two of them. A young man from the community with mental and emotional challenges also lives with them.

The Msibis inform us they will hold church services each evening on their homestead while we are living with them. *Babe* (Mr.) Msibi asks Darrel to "preach" in SiSwati each evening. *I'm glad they didn't ask me to preach! Sometimes there are benefits in being "the wife."* *Babe* Msibi has invited five other pastors and their congregations from the area to join their group for the meetings as well.

Each evening the church grows a bit fuller. Many of the young people lead the meetings in singing and dancing, as well as giving testimonies. Darrel successfully speaks, at least short sermons, each evening in the dark room with the aid of a flashlight. On Sunday, I offer a children's lesson in SiSwati, Obe shares a testimony, and Darrel preaches. Nothing like being thrown into the fire of public speaking in SiSwati. But I guess this is the best way to learn.

I walk into the kitchen the first day to help wash dishes. *Make* (Mrs.) Msibi immediately says, "No, no, the children will do them."

I insist with my gestures, and she finally gives in to my request. When she is convinced I want to work alongside of them, she accepts me as part of the crew and shows me things I can do to help. The family gathers around the firewood stove in the kitchen for warmth, working, and evening chats. So, firewood needs to be chopped morning, noon, and evening. In between other chores, I join the older children in chopping firewood with a hatchet.

Msibi's teenage daughter leads the cattle from the crawl each morning to grazing pastures. She then returns the cattle to the homestead near sundown. Rene begs to go with her, but it would be a long day to keep Rene occupied.

Another daily challenge requires a fifteen minute walk to the hand pump at the community spring. I make it my duty to keep the large water container in the kitchen filled for drinking and cooking. If the Msibi children can carry large buckets of water on their heads, then I can too. After I succeed with a bucket full, I try carrying five liters of water. Unlike the children, however, I struggle to not spill water on the way back to the house.

Sherill determined to carry five liters of water on her head

Washing dirty clothes by hand at the community spring uses different muscles. I wash clothes while bending over buckets, using a washboard to scrub them. After a couple of hours of washing and scrubbing clothes, I am exhausted. While I'm glad to help with chores, I recognize I don't have the stamina of *Make* Msibi.

One day, *Make* Msibi says she is joining the team of men to harvest maize (field corn), and I need to cook the big meal for everyone before their return. *Wait, this was not what I meant when I said I would help her cook!* I explain the best I can in SiSwati, "I'm not sure about using the firewood stove."

Smiling, she says, "I will leave our youngest daughter to help you."

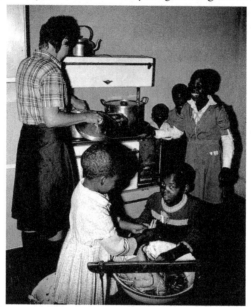

Sherill cooking with the help of the children

In one cupboard, I find salt and curry powder, so I cook the chicken we gave them on our arrival. It has remained cool in a layered "wonder box," a homemade insulated container. After removing the skin of the cooked chicken, my first thought is to give the skins to the cat. *Oh, but maybe the small children will enjoy the skins.* Within minutes, the children devour them.

That decision is validated two days later when we kill chickens from their brood and cook the head and feet along with the rest of the chicken. The chicken heads floating in the pot of food fascinate Rene. I find her scooping out each chicken head with the ladle and hanging the head and beak over the edge of the pot. How entertaining! *Our children are eating the chicken pieces, while the young Msibi grandchildren are eating chicken heads and feet. I'm so glad I didn't give the skins to the cat.*

When the wagon returns with the harvested maize, we all work together to bag the maize before the oxen transport the bags to a wooden enclosure for storage. We then pluck kernels off the dry cobs for hours, resulting in only a small pail of kernels and large blisters on our thumbs. After another hour of grinding the kernels in a hand-cranked maize grinder, we have enough *imphuphu* (corn granules like grits) to make one meal for everyone. What an incredible amount of work just to feed the family for one meal. Babe Msibi will use the services of a community grinding mill for the harvest of corn later.

Returning home with harvested maize and Rene in the wagon

Make Msibi, a petite woman, defies her looks by working as hard as any man. Wearing her long, cotton, floor-length dresses, along with color-ful headscarves, she hoes in the fields, cares for the grandchildren, chops firewood, pounds the maize, and still has a warmth and openness for those who stop to visit. *Make* Msibi also serves as a health promoter for her com-munity. Though she is in her sixties, she walks the steep, mountainside dirt paths to educate and treat medical problems of those in the community. Her compassion and energy seem endless.

Obe and Rene do well at eating Swazi food, although Obe immediately asks me, "Why are we eating with our hands?" This is what we taught them not to do, but to use their spoon or fork. Our children enjoy chewing on sugarcane stalks as a pre-dinner snack. The Msibis offer Obe and Rene a snack of roasted grasshoppers, which is considered a special delicacy for children. Obe wants to be polite but thinking of eating grasshoppers causes his stomach to churn. "No, thank you," he says in a quiet voice.

Rene tastes one and gags, spitting it out immediately. "Yuck, it's crunchy."

Babe Msibi takes time each day to talk with Darrel in SiSwati to en-courage his language learning. One day Darrel is embarrassed by his audible passing of air. *Babe* Msibi laughs and says in Siswati, "A hen always cackles before laying an egg." Clever! We learn that Swazis have many proverbial sayings that they use in conversation. In fact, they don't directly confront one another. They use a proverb as indirect confrontation. In a church service, if a person preaches too long without a break, someone may call out in SiSwati, "My buttocks have now turned sour." And the speaker understands it is time to wrap up what he/she is saying and allow people to stretch.

The Msibi children experience a sense of closeness within their family and church community. They work together all day, often singing as they perform their tasks. After work, the children play in the sandy soil and jump rope as recreation. They have no books, toys, or paper. One day, the three-year-old grandson takes a few of Obe's crayons and places them in a frying pan on the hot stove. He assumes they must be good to eat. What a horrible mess the melted crayons make on *Make* Msibi's pan.

On one of our last days with the Msibi family, Rene chases the donkey the way she has observed one of the Msibi teenagers chasing the cows. The donkey's back leg suddenly kicks her hard in the abdomen. It knocks the breath out of her, triggering a seizure.

Obe comes running. "Mom, Dad, Rene is hurt really bad!"

Darrel runs to Rene and puts his fingers in her mouth to pull her tongue down so she will not be without oxygen. He does not get them out before her jaw locks. Ouch! In watching Rene's seizure, the Msibis are visibly upset and think Rene is dying. They disappear into the kitchen to intercede in prayer for God to save Rene's life. I lift Rene, now limp as a rag doll after the rigidity of the seizure and run to our room while Darrel comforts Obe. He has seen Rene have seizures before, but he thinks he could have prevented this one. Rene cries for an hour after the seizure. I hold her in my lap trying to soothe whatever pain she is experiencing. *How I wish her to be done with seizures.*

Rene and Obe with the donkey that kicked Rene

I am humbled by the Swazi people in giving of themselves and their meager resources. Community people bring chickens and other food to the Msibis for our meals. During the last service, they even give us the offering (equivalent to $8) as a gift of love.

On the last evening, *Make* Msibi is butchering yet another chicken. I inquire about it. She winks, smiles, and says it is for the morning. As we pack our belongings into the car, she brings us cabbages, squash, potatoes, and a roasted chicken for our dinner that evening.

As we say goodbye, *Make* Msibi tells me our stay with them has opened her eyes. "You are just like us and have become true Africans." Oh, how I wish this would be true! From their examples, I learn the true meaning of hospitality and love. We drive home feeling extremely blessed. And knowing more SiSwati. Within a day, Rene asks if we can return to Mankayane.

The Msibi family has become our Swazi home. We spend time with them whenever we can. They include Darrel as a son and me as a daughter-in-law in all the family celebrations.

I reflect that the Msibi's invitation to make ourselves at home with them demonstrates the unconditional love and hospitality of God for us. Amazing. Can I bring someone into our family to be one with us as the Msibis have modeled?

*****

Isaac Dlamini, our closest Swazi colleague, has a small watchmaker shop located near the center of downtown Manzini. We often go to talk with him at his shop while watching him work. He uses a small black magnifier hooked onto his glasses to do the intricate work on the inside of watches and clocks. In a short amount of time, he restores watches and clocks to their purpose once again.

Isaac's deep insight into the heart of God continually challenges us. He is spiritually gifted with an inner magnifying glass for seeing the image of God within people that is often not apparent to others.

"People will change with time, so respect and love them." Isaac repeatedly instructs us. He believes the best about people and affirms the smallest evidence of people's growth. What a wise mentor.

One day, Isaac jokingly gives me a hard time about not going to the all-night services that Darrel attends. I tell him I cannot sleep sitting up, as he and Darrel do in these services.

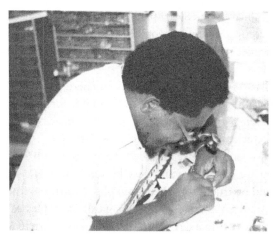

Isaac Dlamini repairing watches and clocks in his shop

"*Babe*, I would probably be like the man in scripture who fell out of the window during the night," I say while chuckling about the story in Acts 20:9.

"*Make* Hostetter, then we would come outside and pray and see God raise you from the dead! You are missing out on seeing all of God's wonders in these services!"

"*Babe*, I claim the promise of the scripture that says God gives sleep to his beloved." (Psalm 127:2)

Isaac laughs, his belly jostling up and down. "I end my case!"

"*Babe*," I ask, wanting to change the subject, "how did you become a Christian?"

"My father lived in South Africa working on the railway for the first twelve years of my life. My mother remarried and my stepfather did not treat me well," Isaac says. "So, I ran away to search for my father."

"*Ncesi* (I'm sorry)," Darrel says. "How old were you when you ran away?"

"Just twelve. It was scary, but I desperately wanted to find my father," Isaac says, pausing his work to face us directly. "I eventually found my father and lived with him, but soon I became seriously ill. The doctor assessed that my lungs were diseased, and he removed my left lung. I was in and out of the hospital for the next year. The doctors told my father I only had up to five years to live," Isaac says, removing his glasses with the black magnifying lens and wiping his sweaty face with a cloth.

"Wow, you were so young to have your days numbered by disease," I say.

"Yes, it was a frightening prediction. That is why I agreed to being trained as a *sangoma* (traditional healer). Others decided that my persistent illness must be a sign that the *emadloti* (ancestral spirits) had chosen me to carry on this role in the family like my grandmother did," Isaac explains.

Isaac stops the conversation to serve a customer who dropped off a clock that had quit working. They exchange family news interspersed with Isaac assessing the problem with the clock.

When the man leaves, Isaac continues, "Now, where was I? Oh yes, my training as a *sangoma*. In the training I heard the words, 'Go, preach, and you will be healed.' But I had no idea what it meant. At that point, I had no understanding of Christianity. I just knew I wanted to be healed, so I left the training, even though it could mean my death. Leaving the *sangoma* training was viewed as dangerous, possibly resulting in a curse on your life by the ancestors."

"That took great courage to leave while not having assurance you would be healed," Darrel says.

"Yes, it did. I wrestled with the decision for months. After arriving home, I had another dream about a blind man who was visiting a neighboring homestead. I found the blind man and during the weeks I spent with him, I was healed. And I learned to know Jesus."

"What a story! We are so glad you were healed, and we can learn from you," I say.

*****

We serve under the supervision and guidance of the Zionist leaders. Working under Swazi leadership sounds like a great idea for us as Westerners. However, we also find it difficult at times. We struggle with the lack of direction given to us. The leadership often meets randomly to make decisions, sometimes on street corners or at someone's home. We gradually grow in patience with any idea we bring to the group. Sometimes we hear our ideas come back as their ideas up to a year later, and decisions and commitments are then made.

Darrel trains Bible teachers to hold classes in many different regions of Swaziland. He joins Zionist leaders in holding weekend trainings five or six times a year at different sites around Swaziland, most often at schools during school breaks. These seminars, open to anyone, include intensive teaching and interaction. I partner with a Swazi woman to do women's seminars. She teaches a Bible lesson while I do a health training. All the teaching is done in SiSwati, so Darrel and I spend much of our time in preparation.

We learn from our Swazi colleagues that leadership development primarily involves relationship building. So, Darrel visits Zionists overnight in their homes around the country, spending time listening to their spiritual questions and insights. These visits become the most meaningful times of mutual sharing and relationship building.

*****

Isaac Dlamini's Humble Acceptance and Love in Rejection

People arrive from all over the country for a weekend seminar at a denominationally owned high school, a three-hour drive from our house. Isaac and Darrel meet with the principal who has made all the prior arrangements for the lodging. The principal apologetically informs them that the local denominational leader is surprised that Zionists are planning to use their facility, and he is asking to meet with them. The school is operated cooperatively by the government and a Christian denomination.

Isaac, Darrel, and two other Zionists meet with the denominational leader on the school premises. After the Swazi greetings, the minister states, "A church group wanting to use the school premises must provide a written application to a committee of the church."

"We're sorry for our mistake," Isaac acknowledges while bowing his head in a gesture of respect and repentance. "We were not made aware of this procedure when inquiring about the use of the school. All the arrangements have been made with the principal."

Isaac lifts his head, shifting his weight. "People are arriving from all over the country and will not have transportation to return home tonight."

"Since the proper channels were not addressed, everyone will need to leave tomorrow morning unless the president of the church overrules our requirement," the leader says, avoiding eye contact with Isaac. "I promise to consult with the president by phone and bring you the final word this evening. In the meantime, you are not allowed to sing, pray, teach, or worship on these premises."

Darrel's anger at injustice toward Zionists rises within him. His self-restraint ends outside the office. "It wasn't our fault that we weren't informed of the proper procedure. How could this Christian group just throw us out and not even allow us to hold our evening meeting?"

The other two leaders agree with Darrel. After pondering in silence, Isaac calmly proposes an idea. "If this church leader will not allow us to have

our teaching session tonight, why don't we request that he come and speak to us instead?"

Darrel can't believe what he has just heard. But they return and invite the minister to come and share a teaching that evening along with his message from the president of the denomination.

At 9:00 p.m., the minister returns to inform the group that they must leave the next day. He then proceeds to give a fifteen-minute devotional on "Don't forget God." Ironic!

The Zionist leaders' behavior speaks volumes. In essence, Isaac is saying to the denominational minister, "We respect you as a brother in Christ," though the acceptance is not mutual. Their willingness to learn from those who reject them illustrates a beautiful example of lavish Christian love and hospitality.

The Zionists trust that another door will open for the weekend. An elderly minister who has never attended one of the Bible classes or seminars stands up and invites everyone to meet in his church nearby. The next morning, the group moves to the church and then holds an all-night service as there are no lodging facilities.

Isaac can receive words from this minister even when his own rights are trampled upon. How often I am focused on injustices rather than creative solutions. I need Isaac's black magnifier to see beneath the surface the image of God within everyone.

Sherill and Isaac Dlamini at a weekend event

11

Giver of Free Will

WHEN WE ARRIVE IN Swaziland in 1983, the government is detaining citizens for protesting. Some are fleeing the country. Crime is rampant, especially burglaries, as well as murder. Less than a mile from our house, two men, thought to be part of the anti-Apartheid party of South Africa, are killed with grenades and machine guns.

The late king, Sobhuza II, died in 1982 after reigning for sixty years. The Queen Mother, one of the wives of the late king, then served as the most power-ful person in the country. She fired some of the cabinet members, including the prime minister. The cabinet replaced her with the mother of the up-and-coming king (the son will be crowned when he turns twenty-one years old). The cabinet members amended the constitution so that the higher court could not question their actions. They also imprisoned the Queen's lawyer without trial.

The political situation continues to deteriorate the longer we are living in Swaziland. So, in 1986, the new king is crowned at eighteen-years-of-age, becoming King Mswati III.

*****

Attempted Car Jacking, 1983

Obe, age five, and I are driving in downtown Manzini. I stop at a red light at the bottom of a hill. Suddenly a man jumps out from behind a bush on the side of the road and runs to my car door. He uses a wire in an attempt to quickly break the lock.

We have been hearing that incidents of car jackings are increasing in the city. I am determined that I will not become the next victim. Although the man standing on the running board of our vehicle almost succeeds in opening my door, I gun the accelerator to the floor. He instantly drops the wire to hang on. As I slow down, he jumps off.

Were we in danger for our lives? Did he have a hidden gun? My mind reels with all the possible endings to this story. Though I have acted on instinct, I am shaken because I could have severely injured the man.

Obe suddenly asks, "Mom, what would he have done if he got inside our car?"

"I don't want to think about it, Obe. It could have turned out very differently."

*****

Violence in the Doctor's Office, 1989

Six years later when Obe is eleven years old, we weave our way through the hospital corridors searching for the Ears, Nose, and Throat clinic. We find wooden chairs filling a small waiting room with blank walls. I take a number and prepare to wait our turn. The room soon fills with patients anxious to see Dr. Ahmadi, the new Iranian ear specialist at the government hospital in Mbabane, the capitol of Swaziland. Before now, we have never found a specialist's help for Obe's ear pain, without having to apply for a visa and traveling to South Africa.

Clang. . .clang. . .clang. A man with handcuffs and leg chains shuffles slowly into the room accompanied by two uniformed guards. They sit opposite Obe and me. I avert my eyes from the glaring stare of the prisoner. *Why is he staring at me? I'm no longer comfortable waiting in this room.*

"Number 9!" The nurse calls.

That's us! Obe and I gratefully enter the doctor's examination room.

"Looks like many battles have been fought in these ears, young man," Dr. Ahmadi declares while examining Obe.

A loud deafening blast startles us all! *Is that the sound of gunfire?* A second blast reverberates through the walls. We then hear people screaming, throwing chairs, and running.

I freeze in panic, my pulse racing. People attempt to come inside the office door. The nurse instinctively throws her weight against the door, slamming and locking it.

Silence ensues.

I am sweating and aware of the thumping in the back of my neck when my blood pressure is too high. My only thoughts are to get out of this place. *I wish we wouldn't have come today. His ear problems can wait.*

"I know your son has had surgery twice already, but he needs it again." Dr. Ahmadi states in an even tone without addressing what is happening outside this room.

How crazy is this? This doctor acts like this is an everyday occurrence! Maybe in Iran, but not here! Does he care about what is going on outside this door? I can no longer concentrate on what he is explaining to me about Obe having ear surgery.

After waiting fifteen minutes, Dr. Ahmadi says to his nurse, "Unlock the door and survey what is happening." He expresses no acknowledgment or empathy for her questioning-raised eyebrows and gaping-open mouth on hearing his request.

As she cautiously opens the door a crack, Obe and I look down the barrel of the prisoner's gun.

"No!" I hear myself squeak out. The nurse quickly slams and locks the door again. *What is going on? Why is he pointing his gun toward us? Where are the police?*

Silence.

Clang. . .clang. . .clang. The prisoner must be walking away.

After more waiting and instructions about Obe's surgery, the doctor asks the nurse to open the door again. This time, the room is empty. She checks the hall for our exit and says the way is clear now. I grab Obe's hand, and we run out the nearby exit.

Safely inside our car with the doors locked, I finally breathe a sigh of relief. I roll my shoulders to relax my tense muscles before driving to the hospital gate.

"What has happened with the prisoner?" I ask the guard who opens the gate for us.

"He held us up at gun point and has now escaped!" The guard exclaims, pointing in the direction the car has taken.

"We're glad to be leaving!" I say.

"Mom, let's chase him!" Obe proposes, his eyes lighting up in anticipation. "I know we can catch him. We have a fast car, and every time we call the police for help, they say they don't have an available vehicle."

"Are you kidding me? We are *not* doing any such thing!" *This son of mine has the same genetic makeup for adventure and risk as his father.*

The next morning, Darrel comes running into the kitchen with the newspaper. "The front-page article is about your experience yesterday, Sherill! That prisoner of fourteen years faked excruciating ear pain, so two guards brought him to the clinic. While you and Obe were in with the doctor, he asked to use the toilet."

"Wow! How did he get the gun?"

Darrel holds up the newspaper and reads, "The guard removed his handcuffs. In the restroom, the prisoner retrieved a gun previously hidden by a conspirator. He pointed the gun at the forehead of one guard, who collapsed in shock. The prisoner fired two shots, hitting the second guard."

"Oh my!" I exclaim. I wipe my hands on my apron and sit down.

Darrel continued reading aloud. "When the prisoner's scheduled ride arrived, he shuffled out to get in the car. Then he held up the gate guard at gunpoint and disappeared. The police discovered where he was hiding and surrounded the house, but he slipped out the back and got away."

"That's too bad. And to think that Obe was sure we could have captured him."

The following morning, we scan the front page of the newspaper for further news.

"Here it is," Darrel says. "The prisoner tried to illegally cross into Mozambique where he was joining others planning to overthrow the king of Swaziland. The Swazi people in the area recognized him climbing the fence. They caught him before the police arrived. According to one report, some police were involved in planning the coup."

"Amazing! Bravo to the Swazi people for their brave actions!"

Darrel pulls me close. "You and Obe were caught in the middle of a planned coup! Unbelievable! Boy, am I glad you were inside that doctor's office rather than the waiting room!"

What a paradox that a place of healing became a threatening place to my son's life.

In Swaziland, I witness many whose lives are affected by crime or violence, whether they are trusting God for safety or not. The Zionists have a different perspective on life, where the circumstances they experience, both the joys and sorrows, are viewed as the means to a deeper relationship with Christ. They do not view God as a cosmic bellhop or puppeteer who pulls strings for their individual lives to be peppered with wealth, health, and security. Rather, they pray about everything with faith, while also accepting that suffering and death are a part of life. They do not take for granted what we in the United States often assume as God-given rights.

12

Companion in Challenges

THE CITY OF MANZINI has a hospital, airport, and an industrial complex. Guests, both Zionists and expatriates, often show up to stay at our house for medical emergencies or business in town. Because of the lack of telephones outside main cities, guests can't call ahead of time. When the bedroom in our separate garage is full and there is a need to accommodate more people, Obe gives up his bed to guests and sleeps on the couch. Many weekends, Darrel attends Zionist all-night services, and I am at home hosting guests. Hospitality for those in need keeps growing as part of our daily life. Darrel assists me with household chores as much as possible. He teaches our Swazi house helper, who works two half days a week, how to make granola so when he is away, she can make it. She usually only has time to do the laundry in a simple two-tub washing machine that requires the clothes to be removed from the wash tub and spun in the second tub. She then hangs the clean clothes on the outside line, and I later bring them in.

Though I enjoy offering hospitality and being with people, the challenge of the unknown of who may show up on a weekend and having food for everyone forces me to adapt. The children and I sometimes make weekend plans, and then guests arrive. So, we try to include our guests in the plans, if possible. When the schedule feels crazy, I long to be with my children, without needing to include others. However, I recognize our children are learning the practice of hospitality.

Sometimes Darrel doesn't return home when he is expected. One night, I wake up at midnight and he hasn't arrived yet. Since we now have a telephone, I call a friend asking for counsel. Do I borrow a car and go looking for him? It requires me to find someone to stay with the children, though. *Perhaps his car broke down or he has been in an accident and needs help.* I wait longer and Darrel finally arrives home at 2:15 a.m.

"Honey, I know you have been worried. The roads were rutted, and I dented the fuel tank on the car. I had gas, but the car wouldn't run. I walked to a hotel to call you, but the hotel had no phone. Then I tried flagging someone down, but the man said he didn't have much gas himself. So, I walked a long distance to get help."

I am grateful he is home safely. My anxiety about him possibly being in a car accident makes it difficult to make good decisions, especially at night. I trust God will grant me wisdom.

*****

Medical and School Stressors

We are grateful to have medical expertise in South Africa for our children. If I trust the medical care, I can take their different medical issues in stride (at least on good days).

Obe has reoccurring ear problems that require a specialist. His ears sometimes develop an abscess, resulting in pus seeping out of his ear. We apply for a visa and travel to South Africa quite often. Ear tubes have been inserted three times; however, they still get blocked with pressure building in his middle ear, resulting in significant pain.

*****

Rene, as a three-year-old, falls off the couch and hits her head on the cement floor. Within seconds, she has a seizure with lockjaw, incontinence, and vomiting, and then sleeps for a few hours.

Swaziland doesn't have equipment to do an electroencephalogram (EEG) that detects abnormalities in brain waves. We finally obtain permission to travel to South Africa for further medical tests after struggling for a week to get a transit visa. The staff try to do an EEG without a sedative, which is unsuccessful as Rene fights them. The nurse then gives her a liquid sedative. Rene spits it out all over me. What she does swallow makes her a bit drunk. We walk outside and carry her around the block for three hours until she falls asleep. She then urinates in her sleep over Darrel. And of course, she wakes up when we lay her on the lab table for the EEG.

Just knock her out, will you? We are exhausted and still haven't accomplished getting an EEG.

In the end, we go to another lab. The nurse promptly gives Rene more sedative and performs the EEG. Rene is zonked for hours, so we lay her in a grocery cart and shop with everyone staring at us. *People probably think we give our children booze and then dump them in a grocery cart to sleep off their hangover. Or do they smell her vomit on my clothes or the urine on Darrel's clothes?* There are so many items we can't buy in Swaziland, and we don't qualify for open visas to South Africa, so we take advantage of temporary medical visas no matter who may stare at us.

The doctor confirms that Rene has epilepsy. He increases her medication dosage, which causes her to sleep so deeply at night that she is incontinent, which psychologically bothers her. I do not want to make her wear diapers, so I wash the sheets every day.

During a trip to a mission agency retreat in Lesotho, Rene falls headfirst into a four-foot cement water trench. She is such a bundle of energy that it is difficult to keep up with her. Rene's fall results in a seizure and unconsciousness, as well as a bloody face from the cuts and bruises. Darrel and I wonder if we are capable of getting Rene to the age of five without major scars.

A visiting neurologist in Swaziland assesses Rene. He suggests I make up emergency kits of medicine to use anally when Rene has seizures rather than having her on a systemic oral drug. So, I make kits for the preschool staff, for home, and for traveling in the car. As a result, Rene is more alert and the sheets stay dry.

*****

Jodie Khetsiwe (meaning chosen to praise) makes her appearance into our family in January 1985, at the local Nazarene hospital in Manzini. When Jodie is born, the umbilical cord is wrapped around her neck and her skin and lips are a bluish color. The doctor prepares to give her oxygen. She suddenly howls and her skin quickly turns pink. An hour and fifteen minutes after her birth, we return home. Obe is six years old, and Rene is four years old, and they delight in pushing Jodie in a red pram (stroller) up and down the long driveway in our fenced yard.

Jodie is such a happy, contented baby, and even when she is sick, it does not affect her positive spirit. I often take her with me to Zionist women's meetings, and she sits on someone's lap during the meeting or is entertained by watching other children.

Before she is one-year-old, Jodie struggles with painful ear infections that keep her up at night. She also has unexplained chronic diarrhea for a year. So, we travel to South Africa to find a specialist for her as well. She doesn't receive a diagnosis, though. We try limiting different foods, but to no avail.

When she turns two, Jodie is hospitalized with a virus that causes vomiting and severe diarrhea. It takes fourteen hours of running an IV wide open before she urinates. This event triggers memories of Obe being so sick in Nigeria. I am grateful that we have better medical resources this time. Jodie recovers from this acute illness and the chronic diarrhea eventually stops as well.

Obe, Darrel, Sherill, Jodie, and Rene

*****

As Darrel and I pray about whether we will return for a second three-year term, the scripture reference of II Corinthians 3 comes to Darrel's mind. He doesn't remember what is in that passage, so we eagerly look it up.

"You yourselves are our letter, written on our hearts, to be known and read by all; and you show that you are a letter of Christ . . . written not with ink but with the Spirit of the living God." II Corinthians 3:2,3 (NRSV).

We sense God desires us to focus on our lives being a letter of Christ read through relationships and involvement with the Swazi people rather than on programs or accomplishments. We affirm another three-year term.

*****

Life Is Not Fair

Rene has seizures for the first six years of her life. When she turns six, her doctor says her EEG is finally showing more normal brain waves in comparison to previous ones. He informs us to be aware that when Rene becomes a young adult, the seizures may return, or she may struggle with a depression/ anxiety disorder. *God, may it never be so!*

*****

Rene has ongoing chronic struggles in school. One day from the parking lot, I hear her first-grade British teacher yelling at the students in the classroom. Rene's initial excitement about attending school disappears like bubbles bursting, leaving nothing but watery tears. She is convinced that the teacher doesn't like her, and she wants to stay home from school.

The teacher, according to Rene, makes her stand outside the classroom if she does her schoolwork wrong. In meeting with the teacher, she admits that she gets frustrated with Rene and thinks she has a learning disability. She recommends that I have Rene tested in South Africa.

Instead, I ask for Rene to be placed in the only South African teacher's classroom.

"Mrs. Hostetter," the Italian principal says, "Rene's present teacher is more qualified than our black African teacher. Why would you do this?"

"We have made up our minds," I simply reply.

After the principal moves Rene to the other class, she returns to being a happy, bubbly girl in school. Her new teacher even allows Rene to talk softly to herself while she does her schoolwork. The teacher tells me that she sees no evidence of a learning disorder. She assures me that she is trying to rebuild Rene's self-confidence. *Yes!*

In second grade, Rene's teachers keep quitting. She has four different teachers in seven months. One of the teachers uses a metal ruler to hit all the children on their open palms when some of the children misbehave.

Rene complains, "It's not fair! Obe and Jodie have the good teachers!"

During that school year, Rene's best friend, Mpho, a Swazi neighbor directly up the hill from our house, dies in a car accident and we are all devastated by the news.

"We've been in car accidents, and we didn't die, but when Mpho is in an accident, God lets her die," Obe says.

"I'm sorry, Obe. Life doesn't seem fair, does it? I don't know why we were spared and Mpho died," I respond.

That evening when tucking Obe into bed, I reflect further with him. "Though I don't have answers about why she died, I do know that God didn't cause her to die. God is not mean and doesn't desire that we suffer. Life is sometimes painful. God will always be with us in hard times, though, no matter what happens. Death took Mpho away from her family, but Jesus took her away from death and she now lives with Jesus."

"If God didn't protect her, how can I know that God will protect me?" asks Obe.

I can't assure him that God will protect us from all danger, like car accidents and death. Isn't that what I'm supposed to tell him as a parent? Isn't that what the Bible storybooks say? Why do I expect God to always shield me from things that others face in life? I must be truthful.

"I can't honestly promise you that trouble will never happen to us. What I can promise you is that nothing will separate us from the love of God, not death, or anything in our lives. So that means that God will always be present with us no matter what happens. Obe, God is caring for Mpho and her family just as God is caring for you in your sadness and questions."

Although Obe probably wishes for a simpler and more reassuring response, he eventually falls asleep.

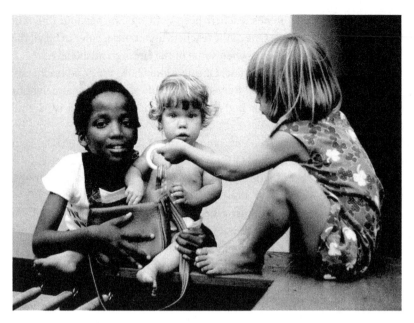

Rene and Jodie with Mpho on the side of the trampoline

*****

I try to control our environment and protect the health of our children. Also, my children being in effective educational environments is a high priority for me. Though subconsciously I have held onto the belief that if I gain enough knowledge to make good decisions and have enough faith, life will go more smoothly in the future, I have learned to let go of this assumption and accept each day's challenges.

I believe life can be difficult regardless of what I do or don't do to prevent trouble. I trust God is present and will offer wisdom in the moment, no matter the circumstance. Maybe the most important prayer is asking God for the inner strength to cope with whatever comes my way.

On days when I am struggling with self-pity, doubt, or fear, I recall a prayer given to me by an Anglican priest I had met in England while Darrel had been studying Independent Church movements in Africa. The prayer, "No Strange Land," by Eddie Askew is comforting to me. Just as Michelangelo has painted a picture of God reaching out to touch Adam's fingers in the Sistine Chapel, so too the prayer offers hope that as I reach out in the darkness for God, our fingers will touch. And I can hear God saying that there are no strange lands as God's presence is everywhere. Where God is present, I'm home.

*****

Rene has great school years in third through fifth grade. I am grateful for all she is learning and the personal care of the teachers. She looks forward to going to school and being with her friends.

In sixth grade, Rene brings home her mid-year exam results. Only fifty percent of her answers are correct. She hasn't received report cards this year and isn't given homework. I investigate what is going on. Rene, I find, has only done seventeen pages in science, five pages in English grammar, nothing in Social Studies, and something other than the syllabus in Math. In talking with the principal, she finally admits the teacher hasn't been teaching and has lied about her lesson plans. The school dismisses this teacher. A permanent teacher is not found, and Rene's class has four interim teachers for the rest of the year.

Rene doesn't want to be home schooled as she is a highly social girl. So, I supplement her lessons with homeschool materials after school. We are all relieved when Rene receives high scores on her finals for the year. With Rene's hard work and discipline, she proves her first-grade teacher wrong; she can do well in school, even without adequate teaching!

13

Suffering in Risky Love

MENNONITE WORKERS IN SOUTHERN Africa are not given visas to South Africa other than transit visas. Based on a cabinet decision in the 1970's, Mennonites continue to be blacklisted due to their peace stance. Whenever we travel to South Africa for medical or work-related reasons, it sometimes takes many days to obtain a transit visa that is only valid for three days.

How ironic that a religious peace stance has become so threatening to South African leaders. The military depends on young white men to uphold Apartheid. Young men who refuse to join the South African army are sentenced to years in prison.

Swaziland is partially surrounded by South Africa, and many Swazis cross the border to work in South Africa, freely traveling back and forth. The South African Apartheid government uproots many South African Blacks from their homes in the cities/suburbs, however, and forces them to move to overcrowded townships designated for Blacks to live. This is allowed in their legal system of segregation and discrimination based on race (similar to how Native American reservations came into being by law in the United States).

*****

Soweto, 1985

One day Darrel travels by car to Soweto, a Black township outside of Johannesburg, with Isaac Dlamini and his wife, Elizabeth. They will be attending an all-night church service in Soweto, the headquarters for their Zionist Church. All foreign journalists are banned from entering Soweto, so any white person or other expatriate seen in Soweto can raise suspicions of trouble in the minds of the government. The army, made up of young white men, patrols Soweto in a declared state of emergency in huge "*hippos*" (armored trucks).

"Darrel," Isaac says, "have I told you the story of when my white friend decided to go with me into a restroom designated for Blacks here in South Africa?"

"No, I don't think so," Darrel says.

"My friend wanted to see what a black toilet looked like." Isaac laughs heartily in remembering the joke.

Flashing lights suddenly shine into the vehicle as an army *Hippo* drives by. The *Hippo* pulls off the road and motions for Darrel to stop. Two young white soldiers with automatic rifles across their shoulders walk up to the vehicle.

Looking straight at Darrel, the one says, "*Wat doen jy in Soweto*?"

"Sorry, I don't speak Afrikaans."

"What are you doing in Soweto?" He shifts the rifle on his shoulder.

"I'm traveling with my Swazi colleagues to an all-night service at their church headquarters," Darrel says.

The other white soldier asks for Darrel's driver's license and car registration. They request the name and address of the church in Soweto. Then they walk back to their army *Hippo* and make phone calls.

No one in the car speaks. Each one is deep in swirling anxious questions of what might happen.

The two soldiers finally return and say they can continue their journey.

As the tensions and violence escalate in South Africa, I fear for Darrel's safety when he travels into the townships. Expatriates in Swaziland tell Darrel it is foolish to travel into the townships during this season of political turmoil.

Darrel is passionate about going to these Zionist church meetings, though. He desires to be present with these black Christians, to share in their sufferings, witness their pain and tears, and encourage them in hope. Many people tell him that he is the first white person to attend their church.

Often while Darrel is in the townships, our children sense my anxiety and wake up from nightmares. I wrestle with God, desiring the courage to release Darrel to do what he passionately wants to do. My anxiety only increases when a black South African friend of ours is killed without provocation in the Soweto township.

"Darrel, I release you to go, even if it causes me anxiety," I voice hesitantly after another long, and sometimes heated, debate about the validity of Darrel's desires. "However, if you are killed, I don't want to be the one to explain your decision to the children. Therefore, before you go again, I want you to write a letter to them expressing why you take these risks and what you want them to know in case you are shot."

Possessing that letter assists me to let go of debilitating fear while he is away. In addition, Darrel writes a step-by-step list of what I need to do if I receive news that he has been killed.

*****

Meeting of 5,000 for Easter Services

"Sorry, there's no more room," the leader of the group tells people who sadly peer into the back of the covered pickup truck with twenty-two adults already packed inside. They are preparing to travel to New Castle, South Africa, for the Easter celebrations.

Arriving at the church headquarters, Darrel is surprised to find the "buildings" made of tin sheeting and a little timber. He learns that this church has been established since the early 1900's.

In 1978, however, after the group had built a permanent building in Charlestown, South Africa, the government tore down and leveled the church building because it was now designated as a "Whites Only" area. The people were moved to the township in New Castle. This explained the temporary-looking structure currently being used as the church headquarters.

There are no accommodations in the overcrowded townships for large groups of people to gather. Roads are not paved, running water is only provided at stations that supply water for a block of houses, and most townships lack sewage systems. Many of the local people live in their own mud, tin sheet, or concrete block homes that lack basic services like working toilets.

During the next three days, Darrel watches in amazement as nearly 5,000 people arrive by bus, car, and truck. At least three cows are killed to feed all the visitors. Little space is available for sleeping during the two consecutive all-night services. The fellowship and worshiping together are far more important than sleep.

After a couple of days, the outhouses are overflowing. And usually on a holiday weekend the servicing of the outhouses is nonexistent. The stench is so strong that it invades every nook and cranny of space. You eat, sleep, and worship with the nauseating stench of sewage, as there is no escape. None of these problems hinder people from celebrating Jesus's death and resurrection, though.

Most of these people are meeting Darrel for the first time. He is blessed by their trust, acceptance, and affirmation. During the first all-night service, Darrel assists the Zionist leaders with the foot washing and communion service. The leaders follow Jesus's example and wash everyone's feet.

The many stories of suffering, harassment, violence, and prejudice people have endured envelope Darrel's thoughts as he washes men's and women's calloused, dirty feet. These feet know the bare ground well, as they walk many miles, suffering heat and cold, and yet they walk in peace.

In hearing Darrel's stories in returning home, I am reminded of the words in Isaiah 52:7 (NRSV), "How beautiful upon the mountains are the feet of the messenger who announces salvation, who says to Zion, 'Your God reigns.' Listen! Your sentinels lift up their voices, together they sing for joy," even in South Africa.

*****

Mozambique, 1986 to 1987

Bordering Swaziland to the northeast is the country of Mozambique, which has a Marxist government. But there are anti-communist forces who are fighting for liberation from the Marxist government in a violent civil war. Their strategies of fighting for freedom, ironically, are often to capture young boys, drug them, and force them to fight on the front lines. For most of the civil war (from 1977 to 1992), an average of two hundred people die daily.

At a clinic two hours from home, I volunteer to treat Mozambican refugees flooding into Swaziland. Another nurse and I sometimes examine sixty patients a day. I learn that one out of six persons in Mozambique is displaced, and I hear stories of civilians being robbed and often deliberately mutilated. The people are also experiencing a famine.

One day at the clinic, I walk up to a burly Mozambican man presenting with fever, headache, and coughing. I think I am commanding him to breathe deeply (*Phefumula kakhulu!*) so I can listen to his lungs. Instead, I say "*Khamula kakhulu!*" I literally command him to take off his clothes. He just stands in front of me laughing. Later that same day, I tell a pregnant woman to pour her urine sample into the car, "*itsele emotweni*," rather than into the toilet (*itsele emtoyeni*). Oh, the joys of speaking in a second language when you are so tired from seeing too many patients in one day!

In 1987, Darrel is chosen as the interim mission agency leader for Mennonite workers in Swaziland and Mozambique. One of the men, Mark, is working on a seed multiplication project in Mozambique. The region has been known as a major breadbasket for the country; however, during this war, a half million of Mozambique's fourteen million people are facing starvation.

One day a massacre takes place by the anti-government forces in the town where Mark lives. The bandits kill four hundred people within ten hours. They enter the hospital and kill every patient. Mark is hiding in a small bathroom where the forces are searching for people in the building. Just before they reach the room he is in, they are distracted by a counterattack by government forces. Mark escapes and transports many of the wounded to emergency medical assistance. He then travels to our home where we offer debriefing and rest.

As I listen to the trauma he has experienced and imagine the horror that he has witnessed, anger rises within me for the utter inhumanity of war. In ten hours, the bandits can kill four hundred people and destroy a town, but it will take many years for people to heal from the trauma and to find hope to rebuild their lives. *Why does God allow such atrocities? How can God stomach all of this? I can't even imagine the survivors believing in a God of love after this massacre.* I struggle to sleep at night as I process the painful stories and the overwhelming helplessness of the suffering Mozambican people.

Mark eventually returns to continue his seed multiplication project in Mozambique. I fear for his life. But Mark is resolute in his desire to stand with the people in their suffering and to assist them to sustain themselves.

*****

Reflections on God in Suffering

As I reflect on our painful experiences in Nigeria and in my family of origin, I put it into perspective with what I have been taught about God. We, as American Christians, often believe that God is our means to security, wealth, health, a loving family, and meaningful work. We pray for our wants/needs to be fulfilled. When we do not receive what we ask for, we question God and try to find the reason why. Or we blame our lack of faith.

God is at work in and through the pain and suffering of my brothers and sisters in Southern Africa. I am challenged by the strong resiliency and courage they demonstrate in trusting and believing that someday they will prevail in finding freedom and justice for all people in their countries.

The genuine suffering love of our Mozambican friend, Father Carlos Matsinhe, deeply moves me. He and his wife struggle to make decisions about him traveling, but he desires to shepherd the people in these hard times of war. His family suffers mentally and emotionally every time he goes on trips to visit parishioners as it means traveling on dangerous roads where frequent attacks happen without warning. Sometimes Father Carolos spends hours lying in ditches or hiding behind bushes while praying that he will not be found.

Father Carlos, along with a few others, risk their lives to help bring peace in the country. They travel into enemy territory to meet with the resistance army's leaders; then they meet with the government leaders. He tells us that after many visits with them, leaders on both sides are agreeing to meet and talk.

Though Father Carlos sees hope for the ending of the war, he is realistic about the needs for rebuilding the country. He explains that over half of the population is now under the age of fifteen and many children are traumatized orphans. Over a fourth of the schools and clinics have already been destroyed or looted. He is praying for discernment on how to be Christ's light in the restoration of the people of Mozambique.

What risky love Father Carlos and his wife are willing to offer in the darkest season of their country's history. They don't assume that God will always protect them when many others are dying. Their willingness to put themselves on the line despite the danger models Christ's sacred heart of vulnerability, to love even when it could mean death. What courage!

Could I do the same? I'm not sure. What I can do is lament to God over the violence and evil and pray for courage to share Christ's sacred heart of love with others, no matter the circumstances.

14

Redemptive Leader

ALFRED MSIBI, OUR SWAZI father, not only provides food to sell and feed his family; he cares for many others who can't afford to pay for fresh garden produce. He often walks the mountainside giving vegetables to others.

Years ago, he developed an ingenious irrigation system for his farm. He dug a canal from a river at higher elevation on the mountain in the direction of his farm. Where there were gullies, he installed pipes so the water would continue to flow with the help of gravity.

Pastor Msibi brings this same learning and problem-solving spirit to the reading of scripture. One day while sitting around his dining room table with another visitor and a congregant, we discuss the Sermon on the Mount and God's desires for us to live out unlimited love in our lives, loving even those who hate us. Pastor Msibi shares a personal story.

"While my brother was planting corn, his neighbor showed up, accusing him of taking possession of part of his land. The neighbor became so angry that he struck my brother across the forehead with a hatchet and then ran off, but not empty-handed, as he helped himself to my brother's fertilizer."

Alfred pours another glass of water before continuing. "I took my brother to the hospital to get stitches. We then reported the incident to the police."

"The man needs to face consequences," declares the visitor present with us.

Alfred continues, "We reconsidered the decision, however, after the neighbor was arrested and put in jail. He would be incarcerated for up to a year, separated from his wife and children. Who will care for his family, fields, and cattle? Who will pay for his children's school fees? Will this neighbor's imprisonment bring peace to our community or divide it?"

He pauses to take a sip of water as we mull the gravity of the bigger picture. "We chose to forgive this neighbor and investigate whether the case could be dropped since it had not gone to court yet," he says.

"Wasn't that risky?" the visitor asks. "Now others will take advantage of you, knowing they can get away with violence."

"We decided to take that risk," Pastor Msibi says. "We visited the neighbor man in prison and told him we forgave him. He apologized for his actions. Afterward we traveled to the police station and asked for the case to be dropped. The policeman prodded us to reconsider as he believed this man will continue to give us trouble. We told him we had made a firm decision to drop the case. We then drove our neighbor back home."

Alfred concludes, "The cost and suffering that came with unlimited love – scar on the head, hospital bill, and loss of fertilizer – was well worth the price to pay for the peace and goodwill that has resulted and is continuing to grow within the community."

Thinking about what is best for the one that has harmed me is so different than focusing on my rights and the lessons the perpetrator needs to learn through punishment. I believe God feels this way about us when we are rebellious. What a challenge for us to practice, though!

Alfred Msibi

*****

Thriving as a Woman Leader Despite the Cultural Views

We meet Hlobisile Nxumalo while traveling on a bus to an all-night service in South Africa. As a lively, outgoing woman, she shares with us many of her ambitions and ideas for the Zionist youth. We learn later that she is only sixteen years old; we are amazed at her maturity and leadership qualities. In many ways, she becomes like a daughter to us. Our children enjoy Hlobisile's visits, and she becomes a favorite caregiver for our children when we are away.

Later that year, Faith Bible School requests our assistance in leading youth seminars. We hold these seminars at different schools in the country during the school breaks in May and December. Hlobisile always attends and encourages many other young people to attend. Participants seek her out for her wisdom and leadership. Hlobisile goes on to graduate from the University of Swaziland in accounting. She willingly serves as the treasurer of Faith Bible School.

Darrel and I often talk about the possibility of some of the youth receiving further training to become leaders of the Zionist youth. We discuss with Hlobisile the idea of sending some youth to the United States to attend the youth training program of our mission agency.

"*Babe* and *Make* Hostetter, please run a training school for us right here in Swaziland," Hlobisile says. "We older youth can't go to the United States for training as we are earning money for younger brothers and sisters to attend school. Without our income, these children may not be able to stay in school."

Eventually, we develop a discipleship training program specifically for the youth. For one weekend a month over the next seven months, we train a group of six youth in our home. Hlobisile doesn't want us to be responsible for all the costs of food and materials. She suggests the youth all pay a small fee. Then she covers the costs of those who are unable to pay. Amazing generosity!

In Swazi culture, a single woman is viewed as a child until she marries. Hlobisile isn't treated as a leader even if she fills a leadership role. She faces the difficulties of being an anomaly in her own culture as a leader in the church. Hlobisile stands tall with her head held high in a culture where single women traditionally have no legal or societal rights. What a tribute to her character.

I sometimes get frustrated with how I am treated as a female leader. But to be treated as a child rather than an adult must be extremely hard, in addition to being a woman leader in a male-dominated culture. Her courage in the face of obstacles challenges me to persevere even when the trials in front of me appear impossible to work around.

Hlobisile Nxumalo

PART III

New Perspectives of Self
Swaziland 1991 to 1994
United States 1994 Onward

The Lotus Flower

Submerged in muddy water
in the lone hours of the night,
the lotus flower laments,
God, how can I survive?
Every night I live in muck,
Yet I'm to bloom each morning?
When will you rescue me
From this toxic wasteland?
Though you don't deliver me,
You offer me a gift,
my petals' waxy layer
protecting me from slime.
With sludge pressing against me,
I embrace the morning light.
My spotless petals bursting open,
sparkling with rare beauty.

—Sherill L. Hostetter

I am the lotus flower.
Because of the protection of my faith and self-image,
I can still bloom in the deepest and thickest mud.
The waxy protective layer on my petals is
who I am at my core,
God's beloved daughter in whom God is well pleased.
The mud of negative messages does not stick.
God is faithful in walking the journey with me,
no matter the risk or the muck.
God is Enough. . .
I am Enough. . .
Therefore, I will Rise!

—Sherill Hostetter

15

Confident Wife and Mother

A HIGH PRIORITY FOR our marriage and family is to intentionally set time apart for Sabbath and relationship building. Darrel and I spend one morning a week reading aloud a section of an inspirational book, playing tennis, and talking together while the children are at school. And every year we take a honeymoon of two nights in a hotel or retreat place. We invite other couples to take honeymoons by offering to keep their children if they will also keep our children for us. It works! Our commitment in this investment is key to our partnership in our family and ministry. Sometimes when we're grouchy, our children will tell us to take a honeymoon as they say we're nicer when we return!

Despite past triggering of not being good enough when Darrel brought up issues in our marriage, I now view our relationship as two persons who resource each other rather than seeking our source of identity and approval from each other. Therefore, we can argue over issues and trust that our love relationship is intact. Darrel and I find joy in spending time together, whether in play or deep sharing.

What a privilege to be mother to our three children. I don't want my own children to struggle with feelings of not being good enough for me or for God. To not repeat the appearance theme of my family of origin, I intentionally work at letting go of my need to be viewed as a good mother and focus on the individual needs of my children.

I keep reading books on parenting. Two books that have influenced me are *Why Not Celebrate!* by Sara Wenger Shenk and *Families Where Grace Is in Place* by Jeff VanVonderen. I pray that I can extend grace to my children and model the love of Christ. Though I often fail, my heart's desire is that they may accept God's grace fully for themselves. Because my mother was often negative in her responses to us as children, I practice being positive and noting strengths by writing notes of love and encouragement and placing them in my children's lunchboxes.

Early in our time in Swaziland, Darrel and I institute a family day on Wednesdays. Our children come home from school to find a special treat I have baked for them. We do fun activities together as well as have a Bible story lesson. I ask our children what part of God's character is revealed in the story as I desire for them to draw close to God as they learn to trust God's character. We sing together around the piano and pray out loud for each other. If Swazi's show up unexpectedly, we invite them to join in with our family time. We don't usually alter what we do because we have a guest. Our family night activities often involve playing games together or playing imaginary school. Darrel and I are the students, and we can be quite obnoxious. If Rene is the teacher, she is a strong disciplinarian. Sometimes, it seems she is taking revenge out on us as parents!

As Obe and Rene grow older, we sometimes hear grumbling about our family night activities, so Darrel and I invite our children to take turns planning our time together. This gives them practice in leadership. Sometimes they invite us to play charades for the Bible story. Jodie sometimes preaches a sermon. Obe and Rene find her sermons to be humorous, but there is always something important to be learned.

Obe, at one point, doubts his own Christian faith. He wonders whether he would be a Muslim if he had been born in an Arabic-speaking country. So, we take all our children to a mosque and request that an imam talk to us about Islam. This opens a lot of conversation for us as a family. Darrel and I believe that our children should be encouraged to learn from others and ask questions in finding their own faith and relationship with God.

For birthdays, we engage in a ritual in which the person being celebrated accepts another year by lighting his/her candle from the Christ candle. We share words of affirmation or scripture with the birthday person for the next year.

One ritual our children love is what we call "honor days." We pick a random day to honor someone in the family. Family members honor this person by giving him/her a little gift or doing a chore in his/her place. In our busy life, this ritual doesn't happen regularly, but it is so appreciated when it does happen.

Darrel is often gone on weekends and some evenings during the week. But he makes intentional effort to be available to the children when they come home from school. They frequently jump on the trampoline together.

They squeal with delight as Darrel forces them to jump higher to the rhythm of his jumping. Ever since being nine-months-old, Jodie has enjoyed flying up in the air and coming back down on the trampoline, with Darrel bouncing her. When the weather is hot, we take the children to a pool nearby to swim. And sometimes there is a special project to work on, like the tree house that Obe and Darrel have built in our tall avocado tree.

All our children have creative imaginations for recreating games they learned in the United States in our backyard. We bowl balls down African mats to knock down plastic bowling pins. Pieces of hard lumber, tennis balls, and hand-dug holes are used to forge a miniature golf course in our uneven yard. Why not have a bit more challenge in these games? It's fun!

The children often build their own houses or schools outside.

Darrel and I realize early on that our children have quite different personalities. Obe is an introvert and sensitive to others' feelings. He is a giver and deeply compassionate. Rene is an extrovert and expresses her thoughts and feelings passionately. She and Obe are conscious of rules, Obe wanting everyone to obey the rules versus Rene often thinking they're not fair and should be done away with. Jodie is a mild, contented child who doesn't express strong opinions. Darrel and I discuss regularly how to parent each child well. We don't sense Obe and Jodie need many rules; we're not sure we can say the same for Rene.

We begin using natural consequences as discipline. I brainstorm consequences that are a natural extension of the choice that one of our children makes. One day while we're preparing to take the family to the pool, Obe uses the hose to put water on the trampoline. We find him bouncing higher and higher with water spraying in all directions like a lawn sprinkler. Obe knows our safety rule that there's to be no water on the trampoline. So, I tell Obe that he has made the choice of playing in water ahead of our swimming time as well as breaking our rules. This results in him not being allowed to swim that day with the family. Of course, that means I need to stay home with him. As Obe and Rene turn into young teens, we explain to them that they have a full bucket of our trust. We will create more rules for them individually if they prove they need more boundaries. This saves us from frequently hearing we are not being fair.

I treasure the time I have with our children growing up. Without the healing in my own life, I may feel more compulsion to do even more ministry *for* God rather than be present with my children overseas. I recognize that if we were in the United States, our children may feel pressure to be involved in sports at young ages. Instead, we have more time together as a family.

During every extended school break, we intentionally plan a family vacation, even if it is a mini one. Most often we go to Durban, South Africa, to the beach. We take in water slides and museums as well. When traveling back to Swaziland, after our times of leave in the United States, we often take mini vacations enroute. As a result, our children have experienced: Jos, Nigeria; London and Birmingham, England; Rio de Janeiro, Brazil; and Nairobi, Kenya. These are privileges we don't take for granted. They are benefits of being in ministry, and they have been pure joy.

We consider it a privilege that all our children attend schools with significant diversity. Obe attends an international school for our last term in Swaziland. Rene and Jodie's school has forty nationalities represented in the student body. Our children enjoy friendships with others from many different cultures and countries. I encourage the children to invite a group of friends over for their birthday parties. For one of Rene's birthday parties, she invites five friends. One girl is from Belgium, one is Persian who had previously been living in Burundi, one is Dutch and had been living in Botswana, one is from India whose family still lives in Gambia, and one is from Tanzania. They look different in some ways, but they love each other and enjoy learning about each other's cultures.

Our children are eager to be involved in blessing others. Near Christmas, we bake dozens of doughnuts, decorate them, and fill new children's size shoe boxes. On Boxing Day, we deliver the boxes, tied with Christmas ribbon, to our Swazi friends. It blesses me to witness the energy and excitement the children have in working hard to bless others.

I'm not always what I would like to be as a mother, but I extend grace to myself when I fall short. I accept the fact that my children may need counseling to process their growing-up years. Instead of believing their emotional well-being is totally up to me, I recognize the reality that there is no perfect family or childhood.

16

Courageous Initiator

By 1991, Jodie, our youngest, begins first grade, creating space for new opportunities. I desire to be more involved in the community around me, along with the seminars I teach for Faith Bible School. As I live into my transformed image of God as one who is all-loving but doesn't promise to meet all my expectations or prevent suffering, I recognize the growing transformation of my self-image. I no longer need to be successful or prove my worth as I'm learning that God's grace comes to me as I am, inviting me to live a new identity in Christ. With my new confidence in God's amazing love and grace, I can risk new initiatives and know that whether I succeed or fail, it doesn't change my relationship with God. And it doesn't need to change my new perspective of myself as I am enough in God's eyes.

So, I volunteer part-time as a nurse at the Salvation Army Clinic. My passion for caring for the most vulnerable has increased over the years. Sixty percent of Swazis live below the poverty line. We begin hearing about the number of cases of the human immunodeficiency virus (HIV) and the acquired immunodeficiency syndrome (AIDS) growing in the country. I can only imagine how this will affect the most vulnerable.

I decide to risk challenging the director of the clinic, Hilda, regarding taking initiative to prepare for the coming AIDS crisis. "The World Health Organization estimates that within the next seven years, one out of every three Swazis may be HIV positive. The suffering we could see in this country is beyond my imagination," I say.

"Well, you might be right. What do you think our clinic should be doing?" Hilda asks.

"My dream is to develop an AIDS education and testing center as well as an education team to go out into the community." Suddenly I'm blurting out everything that's been whirling around in my head recently. "I also dream about persons from different churches being trained as AIDS counselors as well," Hilda's eyebrows rise higher with each new idea.

"Well, you may clean out the storage room on the south side of the building and develop a testing site there," she offers. "First things first" is her motto.

Hilda and I share our vision with others, hoping to gain support. Another mission agency working in Swaziland secures funds for one Swazi nurse to partner with me in the initial start-up. I write a grant proposal and obtain further funding.

The Swazi nurse, Martha, and I advertise our services, and people begin coming for HIV testing. Within a few months, the Swaziland National AIDS Office designates our clinic as the AIDS information and testing center in Mbabane, the capital city where we live. Eventually, the clinic becomes the largest AIDS information, testing, and counseling center in Swaziland.

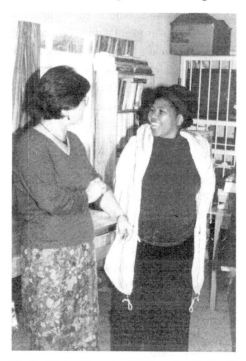

Martha Motsa discussing AIDS work with Sherill

We hold AIDS education seminars for large groups of employees and church groups around the country. Within a year of the start of the AIDS education and testing center, we add a second nurse as the workload increases. In our workshops with church groups, we assist people to look at those with AIDS through the eyes of Jesus. We challenge them to be the hands of Jesus to those with physical, emotional, and spiritual needs.

I'm inspired by the courage of many HIV-positive people we have the privilege to companion. Talking about AIDS is still taboo and those who are HIV-positive are often shamed and stigmatized, and yet they still find inner strength to speak publicly of their HIV status.

*****

Vusi, a twenty-one-year-old male, arrives at our clinic requesting an HIV test because he has continuous physical symptoms. His HIV test comes back positive. He tells us his story.

"I went to a party where I drank too much. A woman at the party I did not know began flirting with me and we ended up becoming sexually involved, though I do not remember much about the night. She called me later to ask if I was feeling okay. When I inquired why she would ask, she just laughed and said, 'Beware, as you may get sick.'"

Vusi says the news of his HIV-positive status is devastating and painful to accept, but he has recently been attending a church, and the support of other Christian friends has helped him hold on to hope for his future, whether he lives or dies. I'm amazed at his positive, accepting attitude in facing his diagnosis as a young man and after being betrayed by the woman at the party.

Vusi opens the door for our team to teach the married couples at his church about AIDS and how they can talk about sex with their children. We also train the youth, with Vusi telling his story at the beginning of the meeting. The youth connect with Vusi's story and ask many questions.

*****

Months later, I receive a request to visit a housekeeper named Alvina. After her husband disappears with another woman, Alvina and her nine-year-old daughter move into a small separate apartment at her place of employment.

Alvina's employer is a professor and an elder in an evangelical church in Swaziland. The employer and the elders of the church receive the news of her HIV-positive status from her doctor before she does. Alvina expresses her pain in how her status has been shared so broadly. *Swaziland could use some HIPPA regulations!*

I educate the professor and his wife about HIV, as they are forcing Alvina to leave her living quarters and her job as their housekeeper. They change their minds and allow her to stay. But they treat her as though she is going to die soon.

On one visit, I find Alvina in bed after hearing she is extremely ill. She admits she is depressed. I suggest she get dressed and go for a walk with me to buy fruit from a nearby vendor. She accepts and feels better by the end of our visit after eating sweet fruit and sharing together.

When the professor and his family leave for Canada for six weeks, another family in the church offers to care for Alvina and her daughter. I'm grateful for this generous offer; however, the family calls her a prostitute and will not allow her to use their toilet.

One day, Alvina stops by the clinic. She states in a firm, confident voice, "I have concluded that I need some control over my own life with a sense of purpose."

"Alvina, we agree with you," I say. "Can we help you in any way?"

"I am going to leave this city and move back to where my extended family lives. What I most need are cement bags so I can build a small house," she says.

I speak with the church leaders about Alvina's request, and they provide some bags of cement. After her move, Alvina sells fruits and snacks to people at a bus stop to earn cash to sustain her and her daughter.

Alvina standing in the doorway of her new house

Ten years later when our daughter, Rene, is working with Faith Bible School in Swaziland in AIDS-related work, she meets Alvina, who often shares her story of finding hope amidst her pain. I am amazed at the health Alvina has found in living with HIV! Rene tells me that Alvina continually expresses gratefulness for the opportunities she has in helping others understand HIV and AIDS. It has given her new meaning and purpose.

*****

Another HIV-positive client is a young man named John. He is afraid to tell his parents about his HIV status. Martha, my nursing colleague, and I offer to accompany him to his home. After driving as far as I can, we hike up a mountainside and walk a narrow path to his house. We don't know what to expect from John's parents.

Neighbors come to greet us on our arrival. We all sit on grass mats outside the mud beehive hut. John introduces us and explains that we have come to discuss an important issue with only his father and mother. The neighbors dawdle in making superficial conversation before finally leaving.

John gives his parents some background on how he met us. He avoids eye contact with them, staring at the ground, as he haltingly tells his parents that his blood test has revealed he is HIV-positive.

At first, his parents are speechless in the shock of the news. We wait with them in silence as they try to process the meaning of what they have heard. His mother sucks in her breath and looks away to hide the tears forming in her eyes. John's father clears his throat, hangs his head, and closes his eyes. After the awkward silence, their questions come spilling out. We try to explain to them what living with a HIV-positive status means for all of them.

John's parents sincerely thank us for accompanying their son to share this sad news with them and being present to their pain. His mother tells me it is the first time an *umlungu* (white person) has visited their area. They invite us to return to train people in their neighborhood. I'm recognizing that caring for people's pain opens doors for further relationship.

As I am leaving, John's mother gives me her handmade, small, tightly woven, red basket as a thank-you gift. I display it in my bedroom where it reminds me how meaningful it is to share in another's pain.

*****

The AIDS team discusses how we can reach vulnerable groups like street children. The many children and youth who sleep in the city park at night don't have a home, or at least a safe home. At Christmas, Obe decides he wants to use his own money to throw a party for the street children. We don't know how many children will come, so it is difficult to plan. We lean on the side of having an abundance of food. Some of our friends caution us about having this party at our home because of the risk of being robbed later, but we decide to take that risk. We get assistance from a few of the children in spreading the word to other street children.

Twenty-two children come to our home the day of the party. We have many games for them that Obe and Rene lead, followed by basketball on our small concrete half court. The children seem to have fun, though they compete over the food and games. We pack the leftover food to send with them as they leave.

The street children eating at our home

Obe and Rene say they are glad we had the party, though they are surprised at how hard it is to have organized activities with the children. We explain to them that since the children live on the streets, we assume they operate in survival mode; therefore, they are not used to cooperative activities.

The party opens the possibility of our continuing relationships with the street children. They always greet us downtown with warm smiles when they spot us, and we engage them in conversation and sometimes buy them food. None of them ever returns to our home for handouts or to take advantage of our reaching out to them.

*****

Faith Bible School asks us for assistance in ministering to married couples as part of the AIDS response. It is cultural practice for men working in the cities to have sexual partners while their wives live in the countryside farming and caring for children. The men go home on weekends and can easily spread HIV to their wives in the rural areas. So, we lead a marriage enrichment weekend with our leadership couples at a retreat center. As a result, a team of three couples is formed to work with us in doing more seminars. They teach the lessons in more culturally appropriate ways, and we buy and cook the food. We hold two weekend marriage seminars a year, and they sometimes hold another one without us.

We want to bless the leadership couples in their own marriage getaway weekend, so we rent a van and take them on a trip to Durban, South Africa, to the international beach where Blacks are allowed. Many of them have never seen the ocean.

Almost all the women don't own bathing suits. Without hesitation, they take their clothes off except for their bras and underwear and run toward the water. The men strip to their underwear as well. The couples hold hands as they tentatively advance deeper into the ocean. Some of them fall when the waves hit them, and they come up out of the water laughing and coughing from swallowing the salt water. What pure joy is manifested in their delight in nature without fear of danger.

17

Believer in God's Redemptive Work

In April 1994, we watch Swazi TV with excitement as South Africans stand in long lines, waiting to vote for a new president. What a joyous occasion for us to have witnessed four years earlier the release of Nelson Mandela from a South African prison! Now, we openly weep as we watch Whites and Blacks sharing umbrellas in the rain as they wait to vote. There are no words for the joy we feel when we hear that Nelson Mandela will be the first black president of the country. Apartheid is beginning to be dismantled!

We listen to Archbishop Desmond Tutu being interviewed as part of the celebration of this historical election. Desmond Tutu is obviously emotional and rejoicing with the outcome of the vote. At the same time, he warns that the work is not done. He reminds everyone that you can officially remove Apartheid from the country, but it is much more difficult to remove Apartheid from people's hearts and minds.

This has proven true because economic, educational, and income inequality in South Africa has not significantly changed as many anticipated. I admit that inequality and systemic racism within the United States still exists since the end of segregation as well. (Recommended reading: *Caste: The Origins of our Discontents* by Isabel Wilkerson)

Archbishop Desmond Tutu with Sherill in South Africa

*****

End of the Mozambican War

In 1993, a year after the war has ended, I have the privilege of traveling in Mozambique outside of Maputo, the capital, with two other women. We visit an orphanage the mission agency helped to establish. Most of the boys in the orphanage have experienced being kidnapped by the rebel anti-communist soldiers and being forced to fight on the front lines during the war.

Part of the skull of one ten-year-old boy is missing because of a bullet. Another boy does not speak due to trauma during the war. None of the children knows where his/her parents are or if they are alive.

The pastor at the orphanage says to us, "The war is over, but we now have a bigger war to win, that of the mind." *How often we, as adults, fight wars and sacrifice the minds and bodies of children! And then their trauma lives on into the next generation.*

*****

Vision of Suffering Love

Each member of our family has been affected by living in Swaziland for over eleven years with wars being fought on both sides of our small country, as well as with internal political tensions and violence within Swaziland. A deep ache of grief has grown within me in hearing painful stories of suffering and recognizing the helplessness many people experience. I wrestle with God on the extent of brutality and suffering in some of the stories, of black bodies being doused with gasoline and set on fire in South Africa, and of young boys being forced to kill their own relatives in Mozambique.

I understand the depths of evil and inhumanity we can lower ourselves to in our claim of "right" causes. Church groups in Florida have provided a cache of guns to the anti-government forces in Mozambique because they were fighting communism in Africa. I try to wrap my mind around the fact that innocent people have been mutilated and killed because of Christians' actions in the United States.

These stories change me. I can no longer ignore injustice, no matter the cause. Scripture speaks about caring for the poor and suffering more than any other subject. Domination over a particular group determined by race or class is never part of Christ's teaching (Galatians 3:28). Neither is violence justified by a perceived right cause.

I am challenged by the South African Council of Churches' work that is instrumental in bringing an end to Apartheid and the misinterpretation of scripture used to hold domination over Blacks. The church has a role in prophetically speaking out against domination and violence, especially to systems of power.

*****

Entrusting Others to Lead

Before the end of our term and our plan to leave Swaziland, the HIV rate in Swaziland becomes the highest in Africa. Martha, my partner in the AIDS initiative at Salvation Army Clinic, takes on more leadership and expands the work and ministry.

Hlobisile Nxumalo accepts leadership for the AIDS ministry in Faith Bible School. She leads teams of youth in using drama and testimonies to train congregations in AIDS prevention. Because of the high number of AIDS orphans, she builds small rooms on her family's homestead to care for AIDS orphans from her community and uses her own income to put them through school.

She also gives leadership to the youth seminars of Faith Bible School. Between ninety to one-hundred-fifty youth attend a week of training each December on their school breaks.

Through difficult economic times, conflicts, and logistical problems, Hlobisile continues to keep the youth as a top priority of her time and income. Though Hlobisile will not be officially named a minister in her culture, she fulfills the role of a minister every day.

Hlobisile's courage in the face of obstacles and her deep compassion challenges me as I think of returning to my own country. Am I willing to take on responsibility for others' care and well-being? Maybe living out the gospel is more about being a "little Christ" to those around me than it is about beliefs or doctrines and focusing on God answering my prayers for my perceived needs and desires. Do we as Christians want a God like this? It's easier to talk about our beliefs and to pray than to love sacrificially.

Hlobisile Nxumalo

18

Observer of My Own Culture
with New Eyes

FOR THE LAST SIX months of 1993, Darrel and I are the interim country directors for our mission agency. The incoming director couple has two small children, and the husband becomes quite ill soon after their arrival in the country. He is misdiagnosed with hepatitis; it is later found to be typhoid after his health declines even further. At the same time, we are preparing for many to come to Swaziland (both expatriate workers and Africans) for a large mission co-agency retreat. This work is in addition to our regular involvements with the Zionists and the AIDS program. We are, therefore, feeling exhausted as we process when it is best for us to leave Swaziland and return to the United States.

Though we hate to leave Swaziland, Obe and Rene need to adapt to living in the United States before attending college. We ask our children to be part of the decision and request they pray about it. At a later family night, Jodie says, "I think God wants us to move to Virginia, even though I don't want to." Obe and Rene express similar feelings. So, we discuss the losses of their friends and schools, and the places they want to visit one last time. We plan on leaving the summer of 1994 and intentionally schedule time to revisit the places that have meant so much to our children over the years. Though we will greatly miss our friends and work in Swaziland, we know we are one in spirit. And we will continue to speak about what we, in the West, need to learn from our African brothers and sisters.

We know we aren't the same people we were when we left the United States in 1983. We are leaving Swaziland with new beliefs, values, perceptions, and attitudes learned through relationships with our Southern African friends. Our image of God and of ourselves has changed. They have taught us the meaning of being the body of Christ in facing whatever circumstances come along.

As Americans, we tend to live with the assumption that what is good for us is good for the rest of the world. We now know that is not true. We need to learn that what is good for the world will most likely be good for us as well. And that requires making the effort to know and learn from the rest of the world.

In living once again in the United States, we are aware that while we appear on the outside to "fit in" with others, internally it is a struggle to authentically be who we have become. In a family night together, we remember and name the joys and the internal tensions we felt when living in the United States on a one-year leave from Swaziland in 1989 to 1990.

*****

Darrel was part-time, interim pastor for a Mennonite church in Lancaster, Pennsylvania. We took advantage of more training in marriage counseling. The small two-bedroom house we rented shaped us further in family conflict skills. The children shared one bedroom with a room divider between Obe's space and the girls' space. We ate at a small table in the kitchen and continued to have guests for dinner and overnight, despite cramped quarters. Making do with the resources we had available is a lesson Swazis taught us.

People at the church were hospitable and accepting. Some congregants became close friends and included us in family outings. Our children made new friends and enjoyed being a part of a musical and other children's activities.

It became challenging, though, when people made assumptions for our family. We only received a monthly living allowance from our mission agency, determined by the cost of living in the country where we were serving.

Darrel came home one day from the church and said, "Sherill, the church is expecting the two of us to attend a Christmas decorated house tour that includes stopping at our church to see how the church is decorated. Here is the price of the tickets. I was told the pastor always participates in this tour."

"What? Why would we choose to pay this kind of money for a tour to view houses with expensive Christmas decorations when we are struggling to even buy our own children presents?" I asked.

"Well, maybe we'll just decline. I'll talk to the leaders and explain why we won't attend," Darrel said.

That same week, Obe got into the car after church and reported, "Mom, the Sunday School classes are all doing a gift exchange. We are to bring a $5 to $10 gift on the last Sunday before Christmas." I looked for small gifts of $5 value to allow our children to participate in this Sunday School activity.

But I felt a dark cloud descend over my thoughts. Do we assume that everyone who attends our churches has extra money to spare? I had recently visited with a new family attending our church that didn't have extended family living in the area. They struggled with paying babysitters to have a night out as a couple. How do they react to these expectations? How do cultural assumptions get in the way of helping people authentically belong in our churches?

*****

After sharing memories of past joys and struggles living in the United States, we process what it will mean for us to return to live in Virginia. In discussing together how we want to live intentionally in a more affluent society, we affirm our desire to hold on to our new beliefs and values and be "joyfully maladjusted." May it always be so!

The Hostetter family before returning to the US in 1994

*****

In our farewell services in different areas of Swaziland, people speak about our relationships with them, being in our home, and Darrel being in their homes. They state specific things they have learned through interactions with us or from observing our marriage or family. In all we are hearing, I conclude that what people truly value is our listening to their questions and thoughts, whether it pertains to scripture, marriage, parenting, or life issues. They appreciate our engaging with them in dialogue. What we are not hearing is what they have learned in our seminars or sermons.

The passage from II Corinthians 3:2 about being a letter of Christ written for all to see comes back to our minds. We haven't in any way been perfect models. We are convinced, however, that our relationships with others is our most significant legacy from our eleven years of living in Swaziland.

19

Receiver of Extravagant Gifts

ONE EVENING IN THE last nine months of our term in Swaziland, we receive a phone call from our friends, Elam and Harriet, in the United States, who have been looking for possible housing for us on our return to Virginia. "We would like to facilitate the building of a house for you in Harrisonburg, and we are calling to get your permission," Elam begins.

"What the world?" I gasp. "Where did this idea come from?"

"I've looked around for a house you might buy," Elam says, "but either the foundation has cracks, or it is too small for your family, or the price is more than your resettlement funds." He continues, "We think building a house will be vastly cheaper for you, and you can then take out a loan."

"You use the word 'we.' Who are you referring to?" Darrel asks.

"We have been building Habitat for Humanity houses," says Elam, "and the thought came to Bernard, my building partner, and me that we could build you a house. We think men from church will volunteer some labor."

"This is beyond our wildest dreams! We are overwhelmed with the offer," Darrel says.

"I think I can get discounts for all the materials, if I explain what I'm doing," Elam explains. "As a contractor, I have relationships all over town."

"Okay, let us talk about it and we'll call you back," Darrel says.

In our discussion, I remind Darrel that I have questioned him on what we are going to do in returning to the United States with teenagers without a house or furniture. In his typical fashion, he usually says, "God will provide." *Could this possibly be God's provision for us? Why would these people want to do all this work for us? It is far exceeding my expectations of God or other people!*

Darrel does not express a need for "roots" in being settled somewhere you can call home. However, after twenty years of being on the move, I am ready for a nesting place. Our possessions are in four different states, and I desire to gather them in one home base. I have cried out to God during past transitions, asking for help to remain content, but I have never dreamed of God providing roots for me in this way.

We agree to the house being built. We pray if this is of God, things will go smoothly in getting the building permit.

Five weeks later, Harriet calls to say, "Your house is under roof already! The block layers donated their time, another man gave a large discount on the cement and then came and poured it, and the church Sunday School class came and worked on Saturdays to frame it."

"Incredible!" I grasp for words. "We are deeply humbled by this out-pouring of love. We don't even know how to thank all of you," I say, feeling the inadequacy of my words to express my feelings.

Elam Steiner and others raising the walls of our new house

Though we don't feel worthy of this love, we humble ourselves to re-ceive this overwhelming gift. Just as we have volunteered to give of ourselves to the people of Africa, many in Harrisonburg are volunteering their labor of love to be Jesus' hands and feet in providing for our needs. What an ex-travagant blessing!

On arrival in Harrisonburg a month ahead of Darrel and Obe, the girls and I hear many stories regarding the building of the house. Except for shingling the roof, the construction of the house has been done with volunteer labor. We will be getting a loan for the building materials and other costs, which add up to half the worth of the house.

Harriet continues to tell amazing stories of unexpected gifts of love. A young man whom we had mentored in his middle school years has volunteered to do the landscaping. A neighbor man has donated a lush new carpet piece for one bedroom. The Sunday School class has held a chicken curry dinner to raise funds for the appliances. Harriet has found furniture at yard sales and has stocked food in the refrigerator. *They have thought of everything!*

On the first tour through the house, Rene and Jodie squeal with delight. Since in Africa we have never lived in carpeted houses, Jodie is so excited about the soft carpets that she declares she will sleep on the floor. Rene exclaims with joy she will finally have her own room. When we get to the end of the hall upstairs, Harriet says, "That's just a storage room. Let's go downstairs and have ice cream."

"I want to see it all first," I reply. I open the door to the room over the garage, and I'm speechless once again. I find, to my surprise, a lovely guest room with its own bathroom.

"We already had the window in when we got the idea of turning this into a guest room, so we removed it and brought the shower up through the window," Elam explains.

That evening as I prepare for bed in our new bedroom, I sit down on the handmade quilt Harriet has pieced and her mother has stitched. I gaze closely at the wall décor Harriet has creweled in matching colors. At the end of the bed lies a crocheted throw blanket Harriet has made to match the quilt. What patience and know-how is needed to make any of these items? I cannot even imagine making all of this as a gift for someone. What many hours of love were stitched into these beautiful gifts! *I will never be able to repay these friends for their kindness!*

We give the house a Swazi name, *Yakhe*, which means, "The Lord built it" or "It is the Lord's." We order a large wooden sign with *Yakhe* engraved on it to hang at the front door as our reminder of God's manna and graciousness to us.

After moving thirteen times in the first seventeen years of marriage, I don't know how to thank God and these friends for the blessing of this house and having roots for the first time since 1974. *God, let me always be generous in sharing this house with others!*

20

Self-Identity as Ministering Leader

DURING OUR FIRST FEW months back in Virginia in 1994, I travel to Washington, D.C. for a six-week course to prepare me for returning to nursing in the United States. Darrel is invited to pastor a local church where he had preached his first sermon at age eighteen.

Eventually, I take a position in home-care nursing. While writing nursing notes in the office, I hear the nursing director speak about her desire for the agency to become certified as a hospice as well. I volunteer to help bring that vision into being by working with the director in writing all the required policies for certification. After we obtain Medicare certification as a hospice, I work as the patient care coordinator of the hospice. Juggling the job with family needs becomes more difficult, though. When Jodie needs one of us to pick her up at school for some reason, I'm often over the mountain visiting a hospice patient and Darrel is in another town in his pastoral work.

So, in 1996, I leave the hospice job and join Darrel in the pastorate at 25 percent time as Minister of Pastoral Care. Though the costs are daunting, I decide to attend seminary. I begin slowly by taking a couple of seminary courses at a time. Through discernment of my gifts, I work toward a master's degree in church leadership with double concentrations in pastoral care and spiritual direction.

On the first day of seminary, the professor asks us to draw a picture of how we see ourselves in this new context. I draw a picture of me peeking out from under the edge of a blanket fully covering me. Though I want to be there, I don't know if it is safe. Too many times, I have had my leadership gifts rejected because of being a female. I have been told women can't teach a class with males present. Male leaders have called me an assertive woman when speaking of my leadership. I never hear a man described as assertive; he is viewed as a leader.

Seminary becomes a healing place for me, and eventually I come out from under the blanket to be who God meant me to be. The affirmation I receive in Seminary shocks me. One professor tries to convince me I'm a gifted theologian; I find that difficult to accept. One day in class, I question him on an inconsistency in his theological statement in comparison to what I have heard him say in an earlier class. He pauses in silence and then congratulates me on being only the second student in his years of teaching that has "nailed him on an inconsistency." Another professor affirms my gifts in inner healing ministry and my depth of listening in spiritual direction.

While in seminary, I read Henri Nouwen's book *The Return of the Prodigal*. I affirm that both the runaway (younger son) and the critiquing part of myself (elder son) need to come home to God in a deeper way. During a spiritual direction session, I sense God wrapping a robe around me and placing hands on my shoulders saying, "You are my beloved daughter in whom I am well pleased." *In my life, I have not heard I am a beloved daughter. And rarely have I felt that my parents are well pleased with me. Can this be true? God said this to Jesus before he started any ministry; God claimed Jesus as his own without Jesus earning favor. That message is now mine as well.*

This becomes a benchmark experience for me on my healing journey and discovering a new image of myself. I am claimed and loved for who I am. And that is enough.

21

Wounded Healer

June 2000 to December 2015

THOUGH WE FIND MEANING in pastoring together, we desire to minister in a more multicultural environment. One of our mentors keeps saying to us, "You are multicultural persons trying to pastor in a mostly monocultural congregation, and you are sometimes misunderstood because of it." So, Darrel and I resign from the pastorate in 1999. We paint houses and clean apartments for a year after resigning to earn enough money to keep the children and me in school and to pay our bills. A monthly support group, led by a good friend, Kathy, journeys with us over that year to pray and discern the direction we should go into the future.

The vision that develops through prayer within the group comes from Isaiah 54:2,3, "Enlarge the site of your tent, and let the curtains of your habitations be stretched out; do not hold back; lengthen your cords and strengthen your stakes." (NRSV). We don't know what this means, but we continue to wait, saying no to opportunities that don't seem to be the right fit.

During this time of discernment, one of my seminary professors promises to join us in praying about our future. One day he says, "Sherill, you only like 'A' grades. But I'm inviting you to embrace three 'C's' in your giftings for your next role: creativity, counseling, and cross-cultural."

"Wow, that sounds like a dream role," I reply.

"I don't envision you feeling fulfilled," he explains, "unless you find a position where all three of these gifts are allowed to blossom."

So, we continue to wait. . .

After nearly a year, we receive a telephone call from the Human Resources (HR) Director of the mission agency that sent us to Swaziland. "We brainstormed a new role that you may have interest in applying for," he says. "It would be an expanded HR role to give overall pastoral care to all personnel, both overseas, and in the office. It will include giving leadership to recruitment, training, hiring, processing of new candidates, and policy."

My heart leaps within me and I can hardly contain my joy. I have shared with a good friend recently that if any mission agency created a pastoral care role, I want that position. We know from personal experience how wounded mission workers can become and how desperately they need nurture and advocates. This role connects to our deep desire to assist a mission agency to pastorally care for those they send overseas.

A week after our interview, the president offers us the position, and we say "yes." I find it difficult, though, to give up my roots again after only six years of being settled. The Harrisonburg house has been a powerful symbol of God's care for my rootlessness, and I can't stop crying while packing. I pray that the house can be a "pay it forward" for others to enjoy. We prioritize making it available to rent to persons coming to seminary or to serve at Mennonite schools or families returning from overseas missions.

In our fifteen years of being HR and Member Care Directors, one or both of us take forty-six trips overseas to respond to crisis or conflict, lead retreats, and/or care for marriages. Despite the long hours of traveling and jet lag in both directions, we find deep satisfaction in seeing the investment we have made into persons' lives bearing fruit in their leadership and mentoring of others.

Our journey is not always an easy one. Bringing change in perspective or policy in an institution with a hundred-year history is not without challenges. We strive to keep the goal in front of us, though, to help create a culture of well-being and crisis care for those who suffer from traumatic experiences.

*****

In our move to Pennsylvania, I begin again with a new spiritual director. I share parts of my spiritual journey with her, including my first day of seminary and symbolically hiding under a blanket. I share my hearing in spiritual direction that I am a beloved daughter in whom God is pleased. She invites me to ask God for a new image of who I am in my role at the mission agency.

Later that same day in a leadership team meeting, the president leads us in a devotional with silence afterwards. In the silence, the image and words come to me.

"The blanket you hid under became the robe of righteousness I wrapped you in. Today it has become your mantle of leadership. So, lead!" I feel a warmth flow through me. *I am in awe, God. How creative! I could not have thought this up.*

Afterwards the President asks if anyone wants to share. I don't want to say anything, as I am the only female leader among seven male leaders, and this message isn't one I want to proclaim to them. Then one of the men sitting across from me says, "I sense God is saying to someone in the group, 'Don't be afraid to be who God created you to be.' Be encouraged." *Did he see something? How does he know?*

He looks right at me and specifically asks me to share. With trembling hands and sweating armpits, I share the image and words with the seven men.

Though some of the men don't believe in women in higher roles of leadership, over time they come to respect my leadership gifts and my strategic thinking. Months later, the man, who had given the prophetic message to me in the meeting, shares with me he has changed his views about women in leadership because of working with me. He says, "I have never known a woman who could do theology or preach and teach like you. My interpretation of scripture has been blinded by my inexperience with spiritually gifted women."

Over the next fifteen years, I wear a long scarf around my shoulders when I anticipate meetings where my voice as a woman may not be heard in the same way as a man's. This is my symbol of the mantle of leadership God has given to me.

*****

As I claim my voice and inner wisdom for both the organization and in ministry with people, I gain confidence in my skills and leadership. I am then able to stand alone at times. In one leadership team meeting, we are asked to affirm all the area conference's documents. I know I can't honestly affirm what is being asked of me and neither can Darrel, but I need to speak for myself. In my response, I explain I can't affirm the document on women in leadership because it lists upfront the conference's underlying assumption that scripture teaches male leadership. It doesn't state any scriptural examples of Jesus or other Biblical writers encouraging female leadership.

I challenge the men to consider that I am leading more interdepartmental teams with them as participants than any of them; therefore, my role does not align with the document. In the end, the request to affirm the document is dropped after a rigorous discussion regarding how women in leadership roles are viewed in the New Testament.

There are times I want to quit over the fifteen years. As I meet with Sharon, my spiritual director, though, I find inner strength to continue to lead. Having a spiritual director while in this role often helps me reframe who I am in different situations and what God is asking of me. My spiritual director models the mothering qualities of God that I didn't experience from my own mother.

My transformed self-image allows me to take risks I would never have dreamed possible earlier in life. Sometimes I need to take crisis trips alone to countries I have never visited, which is stressful. Traveling and sleeping on planes have never been easy for me. With very little preparation, I travel to India alone to offer crisis care to a team after one of the single, female, young adults has been raped while the team is on vacation. The long-term mission leaders in the area need to travel to lead a training elsewhere, so they leave the day after I arrive. On jet lag, I debrief the team, spend time alone with the traumatized female, and make plans for further healthcare for her. Though I am exhausted, my passion for caring well for traumatized workers energizes me, and God grants me inner strength.

After deciding together with supervisors and the members of this team that they will return to the United States, I work with them on what closure of their assignment will look like and what priorities are important for them personally. They all desire to see the Taj Mahal before leaving Asia, so we travel together to witness this world wonder. Afterwards, the girls and I travel on an overnight train back to their place of ministry to say goodbye and to gather their personal belongings. On the train, we have a designated sleeping compartment of stacked beds, sleeping twelve. The compartment is open to mixed-genders, and after all twelve beds are accounted for, we realize that we are the only women. Private sleeping compartments are very limited and quite expensive. We have no choice at this late notice. I assure the girls I will remain awake until all the men have fallen asleep. After traveling back to the United States with all five of the team members, I then meet and talk further with the parents at the airport before finally being able to let down in my own home.

Sleeping doesn't come easily for me in other beds, and on fast-paced trips, I sometimes don't even have a bed to sleep in. Though I don't sleep well for quite a few nights and the trip and work in crises are stressful, I trust God to show up and grant me wisdom. And I celebrate that I can do ministry that doesn't have a guidebook for the exact techniques to deal with unique crises. Each crisis has its own dynamics and relationships to consider. With my transformed self-identity, I no longer need to know exactly how to do something in order to take a big risk. I now go with the flow, trusting my own intuition, wisdom, and the Spirit of God within me.

My life verse of Philippians 3:10 says, "I want to know Christ and the power of his resurrection and the sharing of his sufferings. . ." (NRSV). Earlier in life I have desired the power of the resurrection to prevent and rescue me from suffering. But it is the power of Christ's resurrection that gives me courage and strength to share with Christ in suffering love and justice for all.

In my journal I write my vision of trust:

Thanksgiving for what I have;

Relinquishing what is not mine to control;

Untethering from catastrophic thinking;

Surrendering to the mystery of God;

Turning to God for light and peace.

*****

After Darrel has an extensive and complicated heart ablation surgery in January 2015, the surgeon tells us it's time to allow younger persons to do our jobs, as the fast-paced and intensive overseas trips we make are taking a toll on our bodies. In leaving our roles at the end of 2015, we name what a privilege it has been to journey with mission workers through many sacred conversations about their individual or marital struggles, inner wrestling in relation to God, or the challenges in their ministry. We have found deep meaning in journeying with those who have been traumatized overseas and advocating for their needs in finding healing. There have been many tasks to be accomplished in our role, but the relationships we have built with workers have become the most important work.

As trained spiritual directors, Darrel and I have heard many people struggling with their image of God or their self-image. We have found deep joy and meaning in assisting persons as spiritual midwives to notice the healing and new growth God is birthing within them.

22

Releasing and Blessing

IN OCTOBER 2002, ON a personal silent retreat, I'm meditating under a large weeping willow tree, embracing its strength and beauty. Its branches hang low to the ground and remind me of the symbol in scripture of finding rest and refuge beneath God's wings (Psalms 36:6; 61:4; 91:24). The weeping willow tree invites me to come inside its branches and find rest for my soul.

The tree wraps its arms around me as I reflect on turning fifty and grieving my mother being in an Alzheimer's unit. She will not be living much longer on earth. As I pray for my mother, I grieve the loss that she has not been healed psychologically and emotionally in this life prior to dealing with Alzheimers.

I have expected life to be like an apple tree, always giving me nourishment and goodness. Most trees grow branches that reach to the sky, giving fruit or flowers or nuts in their season. When this has not been my reality, I often have become angry and distraught. However, God has brought me a different dream, that of living under the weeping willow.

This tree adapts to any soil type or drought. It grows up to ten feet per year, creating an oasis of shade in any environment. Salicylic acid, found in its sap, grants aspirin its pain-relieving quality. The tree and its sap promote rest and healing.

The branches gently blow across my back, stroking me, encouraging me to embrace my life under the weeping willow. My heart fills with gratitude as I dream of inviting others to meet me under my weeping willow tree. Together we will encounter God while being held in the long, loving branches.

I can be a wounded healer under the weeping willow tree, rather than wishing to be an apple tree that gives juicy red apples to delight others. Though my life story is different from others, I don't need to follow conventional patterns through life. I desire to be one who can weep with those who weep. Therefore, I will continue to embrace the weeping willow tree as my place to live. In this space, I will marvel at the wonders of God beneath the healing branches.

*****

Letter Written Years after Mother's Death at Age Seventy-nine

Dear Mother,

You are now gone from this earth, and I trust you are finally full of joy in heaven.

When we spent time sorting through your personal items, I saved your black leather Bible with your name engraved in gold lettering on the outside. I did not want any of your collections of beautiful things you displayed in your home. I wanted to save something of who you really are as a person. I looked through the pages of your Bible for any clues about your inner being, but I found nothing. No handwriting of your name on the designated page. No highlighting or underlining of verses that held meaning for you. Nothing. At. All.

I have longed as an adult to know your love, your passions, your deeper thoughts about life itself. But it is not to be. I continue to long for memories of you cuddling me, reading books to me, speaking your love to me. If they are in the reality of time past, I haven't been able to conjure them to the surface. Some of the positive memories I do have are ones that my siblings don't remember, and sometimes I have been accused of making them up. I grieve that I don't know you as a person.

What was behind the veil of your mental illness? What did you delight in? What were your dreams? What memories did you treasure? When I interviewed you, Mother, I learned a few things about your life I wish had been different for you.

I grieve that your father had forced you to quit school by eighth grade and work in the fields. I am sorry you were bullied by your brothers who were older and stronger. I grieve the life you didn't have, the opportunities you were never given. *You desperately wanted to feel loved by others. You probably never understood why others distanced themselves from you when they experienced your attempts to be loved as manipulation.*

I grieve the mental illness you lived with and the lack of treatment for your symptoms. *Your paranoia prevented you from trusting doctors or us in getting you help. And we weren't trained in how to gain your cooperation. Dad did not want to "rock the boat," as he also feared your responses.* I grieve Dad enabling you in your illness rather than protecting us as children.

Mother, I dreamed often of having an intimate and close relationship with you. That dream over time became a "never will be," a death, a letting go.

Alzheimer's disease placed a thicker veil between us. It felt cruel to place you in a locked facility for your last six years. Dad had come to the end of his coping, though. You kept him up at night, pulling his hair, and hitting him. When you threatened to kill him with the kitchen butcher knife, he left home without shoes or glasses and drove around town until morning. We had to intervene.

When I visited you at the facility, you kept repeating, "I know you're responsible for my being here, Sherill. I pray God will punish you for what you've done to me." Each time I heard it, the knife tore a bit deeper within my heart. There was no way to reason with you or try to explain. You could not understand.

The last few times I visited you, conversation was difficult. "How come you're only now coming to visit me? How long have you been here and not shown up to see me?" you asked me each day. I explained that I had come every day I had been in town, but nothing was remembered. Conversation with you evaporated into the air. I suggested we sing together. We sang the hymn "Blessed Assurance." You remembered every word of the song. You lifted your arms in the air and closed your eyes. Your body relaxed and appeared as peaceful as I had ever seen you. You were communing with the God you knew. How ironic that I as your daughter could not connect with you, although we could both connect with God in ways that calmed and quieted our souls. Communion in the Spirit!

God assured me that day, "She can forget her own name, but I will always know her by name. I am covenanted to your mother forever. Can you entrust her to me?"

Although your paranoia and anger became more prominent in your last six years, I treasure the pearl that also shone forth. Your confused mind took you back to memories of being in the hospital after giving birth to me.

When Dad came to visit, you were often focused. "Glen, go find Sherill. I don't know why the nurses won't bring my baby back to me. Go get her so I can feed her." You kept repeating it until Dad agreed and walked down the hall.

"Sherill is peacefully sleeping," he would say on his return, "and the nurses say it is not time to feed her yet." Hearing this story brought me the sense of your love beneath the veil.

As you were dying, I visited you daily. Though the young staff nurse told you to keep fighting, assuring you that you could beat death and live longer, I assured you of our love. I read Psalm 23 to you and invited you to take Jesus' hand as your shepherd, allowing Jesus to lead you to heaven. Miriam and I promised you there was nothing to fear. After singing "Blessed Assurance," we left, as it was late in the evening. An hour later, you took your last breath. You believed me in your last hours and trusted my counsel.

You carried me within yourself and brought me into life and gave me my name. Thank you! For how you cared for me in the ways you were capable, thank you. You sewed clothes for me and my dolls and made sure we weren't hungry. You valued me receiving a good education. Thank you!

I have seen you, heard you, touched you as my mother, but as a child who has tried hard to please you and prevent your rage. I have feared your reactions. I grieve not having a deeper relationship in knowing you and being known by you.

I wonder who you may have become if you had the opportunities I did in life? If you could have received treatment for your mental illness, what might we have talked about while sitting across from each other at a cozy café? What memories would we have enjoyed laughing about? I hope to know someday.

Though your black leather Bible is blank inside, lacking any clues about you, it still has your name engraved on the front. It belongs to you. Through the veil of your mental illness, I know you loved me. You and I share common obstacles that robbed us both of a relationship we longed for but could never obtain. Knowing our mutual longing has brought comfort and hope for someday when the veil will be torn asunder. We will truly see and know each other beyond our names and limited memories.

I love you,

Sherill

*****

Reconnecting In Jubilee Year

In 2001, Darrel enters his fiftieth year. As his Jubilee year, he meditates on the scriptural reference to jubilee (Leviticus 25:8–12), a year of rest every fifty years to acknowledge God's provision and forgive all debts. He embraces the invitation of reflecting on the past and releasing any further emotional debts. We invite the leadership of the mission agency that sent us to Nigeria, the delegation that came to visit us on-site, and the principal of the school in Nigeria to have more reflective conversation with us on what had happened over twenty years earlier.

Only the couple on the delegation responds positively to our invitation. They are planning to travel through our town on a trip, so the opportunity to meet in person is welcomed. In our retelling of our stories, they explain they had not received an orientation about our situation in Nigeria prior to their arrival.

We validate the statement they had written in the report saying, "this experience will affect Darrel and Sherill the rest of their lives." We share with them how our experiences in Nigeria led to our passion for member care for mission workers and the deep joy and meaning we have found in our ministry.

In our time together, we listen to each other's stories, cry together, and extend grace, hugs, and reconciliation. We find the experience to be a deeper healing from the Nigerian experience that had originally brought us together over two decades earlier.

Later, we learn that the mission agency that sent us to Nigeria now has their own member care focus. Therefore, our story will likely never be repeated.

23

Letting Go of Past Decisions

AGAINST ALL OUR WISHES and prayers, Rene does become depressed in college. We try to give her the support and resources she needs, but she is in Kansas, and we are in Pennsylvania.

Over the two years she is in Kansas, I struggle to deal with my own emotions in listening to her pain. The current reality takes me back to Nigeria and not having sunlight to deal with her high bilirubin. But berating myself for our decision to give birth in Nigeria benefits no one now.

I wonder some days whether I will receive a phone call telling me that Rene has taken her own life. Darrel assures me, "I am convinced God is at work in Rene and God is walking with her. We can trust this journey will end in life, not death."

After graduating from a two-year college in Kansas, Rene transfers to Eastern Mennonite University in Harrisonburg, Virginia. But the transition is difficult, as she has lost her friends.

On one phone call, I sense she may be having suicidal ideation. My chest tightens and a sense of heaviness engulfs me. I convince her to go to the hospital for help, and she is admitted. We leave Pennsylvania and visit her in the hospital in Virginia. The nurse tells us visitors are only allowed for one hour twice a day. She encourages us to come back on the weekend after she has been in treatment for a few days. Rene, instead, is discharged from the hospital in a short period of time without anyone being notified. After she is discharged from the hospital, I don't hear from her, and she doesn't answer her phone. Obe goes to her apartment, breaks in, and finds her lying in bed with a whole bottle of medicine poured out on her side table. He convinces her to come with him to his house.

After hearing from Obe, I mull the best response. "Darrel, I believe Rene needs you in this crisis rather than me. If we both go, she will gravitate to me, but I sense that Rene needs you to represent Christ's unconditional love for her." As a teenager, she had critiqued Darrel as being more of the disciplinarian in the family.

Obe succeeds in keeping Rene at their apartment for the next four hours until Darrel arrives. Darrel walks inside and wraps his arms around Rene, saying nothing. They cry together in each other's arms in silence. Darrel then tells Rene nothing can change the love he has for her, as she will always be his beloved daughter. He brings her back to Pennsylvania, and we secure more emotional support for her.

In walking this journey with our daughter, the challenge each day involves letting go of control of all we can't fix for her. I continually pray Rene will learn to fly again.

Following college, she serves for two years in Swaziland, teaching and living with AIDS orphans, as well as working with Faith Bible School. After returning to the United States, she attends seminary. Later, she pastors two different churches and is currently the palliative care chaplain for the local hospital and an end-of-life doula. Patients and families she cares for tell her what a gift she is as she establishes emotional rapport almost immediately and helps them talk about their fears, anger, grief, and loss. God has transformed her pain into beauty and giftedness beyond our wildest dreams.

The pain my daughter has endured cuts deeper than my own past pain. I often think I will be able to protect my children from having emotional pain of never being good enough or believing lies about themselves. But I fail! Rene has cried out to God so often but continues to struggle at times with anxiety.

I realize that God can't always protect me from pain and loss connected with the actions of others. Otherwise, he would be a puppeteer God rather than the God we know. In the same way, I, as a parent, can't always protect my own daughter. It isn't that I don't care enough to do something about it. I care deeply. But I care enough to allow her to make her own decisions, assuring her we will support and love her no matter what she decides.

Rene as an adult

24

Mystery

THE IMPRINTED IMAGE OF God from my childhood was God as our impenetrable shield from evil and suffering. I knew with certainty the character of God and the promises in scripture of how God would act. Life, however, brought trauma, chaos, and difficulties. My certainty unraveled through the suffering and complexities of life. These experiences didn't align with my view of God, leaving me perplexed. I engaged the doubts and questions and opened myself to learn from those who viewed life differently. Gradually, my understanding of God and myself changed. Rather than expecting certainty in taking risks in life, I learned that all of life is the means to a deeper joyous and mysterious relationship with God.

Certainty, complexity, perplexity, mystery. . . These are the cycles of learning and wisdom that keep me from becoming dogmatic and hard-hearted. It is freeing to let go of demanding surety and be able to live with some unanswered questions while trusting our mysterious God more fully. I now live with deep gratitude for life itself and all the gifts in life that I enjoy.

The journey of my life has been one of riding over varied terrain: flat and open; rocky and inhospitable; wild and adventurous; treacherous and hostile; jagged and barren; meaningful and fulfilling. Sometimes, all I can do in the ups and downs of the journey is keep my balance and stay in the saddle of the thoroughbred as I continue to ride across the terrain.

Balance requires a strong core, and my God image and self-image establish that core. My perceptions, attitudes, and behaviors stem from my core. As I have traveled through life, my core has been transformed, resulting in seeing with new eyes, both the beauty and the pain. Even in the shadow of death, I trust my Creator to envelope me with divine presence and peace.

When I find myself knocked off center due to life experiences, I remain open to God's love and presence. I trust there is no loss or fear or death so deep that God's presence can't eventually be perceived. God offers us life whether we experience a rescue or a miracle or new life through death itself. God can be found in our uncertainties, and comfort experienced in our anguish and questions.

The challenge as I age and ride into the future is to stay open to God's Spirit in discovering the magnificent geography and people around me. Openness to learn requires an awakened curiosity and courage to ask questions. Eventually, it leads me to a deeper awe of God.

What a wild and beautiful ride!

And onward I go. . .

Darrel and Sherill Hostetter, Fall 2021

More pictures and poems related to this story
can be found at https://wildridebook.com

Made in the USA
Middletown, DE
01 July 2022

68253131R00096